D0528591

SCI-FI MOVIES

FACTS, FIGURES & FUN

*"Any book without a mistake in it
has had too much money spent on it"*
Sir William Collins, publisher

SCI-FI MOVIES

FACTS, FIGURES & FUN

JOHN GRANT

ff&f

For Randy and Barbara Dannenfelser

Sci-Fi Movies
Facts, Figures & Fun

Published by
Facts, Figures & Fun, an imprint of
AAPPL Artists' and Photographers' Press Ltd.
10 Hillside, London SW19 4NH, UK
info@ffnf.co.uk www.ffnf.co.uk
info@aappl.com www.aappl.com

Sales and Distribution
UK and export: Turnaround Publisher Services Ltd.
orders@turnaround-uk.com
USA and Canada: Sterling Publishing Inc. sales@sterlingpub.com
Australia & New Zealand: Peribo Pty. peribomec@bigpond.com
South Africa: Trinity Books. trinity@iafrica.com

A catalogue record for this book is available from
the British Library.

ISBN 13: 9781904332350
ISBN 10: 1904332358

Design (contents and cover): Malcolm Couch
mal.couch@blueyonder.co.uk

Printed in China by Imago Publishing
info@imago.co.uk

For information about custom editions, special sales, premium
and corporate purchases, please contact ffnf Special Sales
+44 20 8971 2094 or info@ffnf.co.uk

CONTENTS

The EDISON
KINETOGRAM

VOL. 2   MARCH 15, 1910   No.

SCENE FROM
FRANKENSTEIN

FILM No. 6604

EDISON FILMS RELEASED FROM
MARCH 16 TO 31 INCLUSIVE

AND WHAT DO YOU MEAN BY SCI-FI?

For written texts of science fiction, the term "sf" or "SF" is vastly preferred to "sci-fi", which, often pronounced "skiffy", is a term of derogation, affectionate or otherwise: it refers to *bad* science fiction. However, "sci-fi" is in universal use without that connotation in the context of sciencefictional movies, and is used thus here.

Of course, the vast majority of sci-fi movies would still be skiffy if translated into print.

Why?

Hollywood has never really understood the appeal of sf, and has been terrified that audiences will be frightened off by all these danged *concept* thingies. Consequently, producers have tended to insist on substituting sensation, spaceship chases (like car chases, but . . .) and loud explosions (even in a vacuum) for science fiction's main stock-in-trade: ideas. This became even more the case after the release of *Star Wars* in 1977, and the attitude has been largely unaffected by the success of more thoughtful commercial pieces like *Blade Runner* (1982), *The Handmaid's Tale* (1990) and *12 Monkeys* (1996). A culmination came in 2005 with *I, Robot*, which not only had virtually nothing to do with the Isaac Asimov fiction upon which it was supposedly based but also had, as a key plot element, robots disobeying Asimov's famed Three Laws of Robotics: how could there be a standard-issue Will Smith shoot-em-up if the robots were incapable of killing people?

In short, the sci-fi movie has over the past few decades

diverged quite considerably from written sf; it would hardly be unfair to describe the two as separate but overlapping genres.

At its best – and *Star Wars* is a good example – the sci-fi actioner can be tremendous fun. At its worst . . . well, that's another story. Some of the sci-fi movies mentioned in this book are also good sf. Plenty are bad sf but are good sci-fi movies. And some are bad sf *and* bad sci-fi – and they can be the most fun of all.

A Note on Terminology
I have borrowed two abbreviations from the Clute/Nicholls *Encyclopedia of Science Fiction* and the Clute/Grant *Encyclopedia of Fantasy* (see Bibliography):
"vt" stands for "variant title"
"dir" stands for "directed by"

A Note on Straplines
Scattered throughout the text are movie-poster straplines (or taglines) that have caught my fancy. Some are delightfully cheesy; others somehow capture what the joys of watching sci-fi movies are all about.

Aliens Resurrecting the Dead! Flying Saucers Over Hollywood!
Plan 9 from Outer Space (1959)

Futureworld –
Where You Can't Tell the Robots from the Machines
Even When You Look in the Mirror!
Futureworld (1976)

THEY SPAWNED
SCI-FI MOVIES:
THE DIRECTORS

Not every movie director has dabbled in sci-fi, but a surprising number have, and some have made it their life's work. Here are a few who are especially associated with the field, together with selective filmographies.

TIM BURTON (b1958)

One of the quirkiest of Hollywood's frontline directors. His career, which has been marked throughout by an interest in fantastication, began as an animator at Disney, where, extraordinarily, after an apprenticeship on their orthodox features he was allowed to do his own thing, making the shorts *Vincent* (1982) and *Frankenweenie* (1984). Pee-Wee Herman saw the latter, which is live-action, and insisted Burton direct *Pee-Wee's Big Adventure* (1985). After that there was no looking back. The stop-motion-animated movie *Tim Burton's The Nightmare Before Christmas* (1994) was dir Henry Selick, although very much Burton's baby.

Tim Burton: Select Filmography

1988: *Beetle Juice*
1989: *Batman*
1990: *Edward Scissorhands*
1992: *Batman Returns*
1994: *Ed Wood*
1996: *Mars Attacks!*

1999: *Sleepy Hollow*
2001: *Planet of the Apes*
2003: *Big Fish*
2005: *Charlie and the Chocolate Factory*
2005: *Corpse Bride*

JAMES CAMERON (b1954)

Canadian-born US director whose first job in cinema was on Roger Corman's *Battle Beyond the Stars* (1980) but who has since become known for his large-budget blockbusters, many of which have been sci-fi (1997's *Titanic* is an example of one that is not). His first big movie was *The Terminator* (1984), which he co-wrote.

James Cameron: Select Filmography

1978: *Xenogenesis*
1981: *Piranha Part Two: The Spawning*
1984: *The Terminator*
1986: *Aliens*
1989: *The Abyss*
1991: *Terminator 2: Judgment Day*

JOHN CARPENTER (b1948)

US director who has always been associated with the fantastic and horror. He first made his mark with *Dark Star* (1974), a satirical pre-emptive counter to movies like *Star Wars* (1977). He is also a writer and musical (soundtrack) composer. Many of his movies have been retitled with the prefix *John Carpenter's* ...

John Carpenter: Select Filmography

1974: *Dark Star*
1978: *Halloween*
1980: *The Fog*
1981: *Escape from New York*

1982: *The Thing*
1983: *Christine*
1984: *Starman*
1986: *Big Trouble in Little China*
1987: *Prince of Darkness*
1988: *They Live!*
1992: *Memoirs of an Invisible Man*
1994: *In the Mouth of Madness*
1995: *Village of the Damned*
1996: *Escape from L.A.*
1998: *Vampires*
2001: *Ghosts of Mars*

DAVID CRONENBERG (b1943)

Canadian-born US director whose fascination with the processes of the flesh has meant he has never been far from controversy, with some of his movies being condemned as porn. Leaving aside the hoohah, however, he has been one of sci-fi cinema's most consistently interesting directors.

David Cronenberg: Select Filmography

1970: *Crimes of the Future*
1975: *Shivers*
1977: *Rabid*
1979: *The Brood*
1981: *Scanners*
1983: *Videodrome*
1983: *The Dead Zone*
1986: *The Fly*
1988: *Dead Ringers*
1991: *Naked Lunch*
1996: *Crash*
1999: *eXistenZ*
2002: *Spider*

ROLAND EMMERICH (b1955)

German-born US director, nicknamed in his homeland Das Spielbergle aus Sindelfingen ("Sindelfingen's Little Spielberg"), who has made a string of often critically disliked but nonetheless highly watchable sci-fi blockbusters.

Roland Emmerich: Select Filmography

1990: *Moon 44*
1992: *Universal Soldier*
1994: *Stargate*
1996: *Independence Day*
1998: *Godzilla*
2004: *The Day After Tomorrow*

STANLEY KUBRICK (1928–1999)

US-born director best known for the work he did in the UK; his relatively few movies included three core to the sci-fi genre. At the time of his death he left unfinished (in fact, barely started) *A.I.: Artificial Intelligence*, which was completed by Steven Spielberg.

Stanley Kubrick: Select Filmography

1964: *Dr. Strangelove, or How I Learned to Stop Worrying and Love the Bomb*
1968: *2001: A Space Odyssey*
1971: *A Clockwork Orange*
1980: *The Shining*
1999: *Eyes Wide Shut*
2001: *A.I.: Artificial Intelligence* (unfinished)

GEORGE LUCAS (b1944)

Lucas's life was changed when he won a scholarship to watch the filming of Francis Ford Coppola's fantasy *Finian's Rainbow* (1968); the two men became friends, and the following year founded American Zoetrope, whose first movie was also Lucas's first sci-fi feature: *THX 1138* (1971). Since then he has become known almost exclusively for the *Star Wars* movies and for his visual-effects company Industrial Light & Magic.

George Lucas: Select Filmography

1971: *THX 1138*
1973: *American Graffiti*
1977: *Star Wars*
1999: *Star Wars: Episode I – The Phantom Menace*
2002: *Star Wars: Episode II – Attack of the Clones*
2005: *Star Wars: Episode III – Revenge of the Sith*

GEORGES MÉLIÈS (1861–1938)

French pioneer of the cinema, who began as a conjurer and carried his interest in tricks into motion pictures. Of his over 550 known movies, a high proportion were sciencefictional or otherwise fantasticated, including *Le Voyage dans la Lune* (1902) which, at 21 minutes (when most movies were lucky to last five minutes), can be regarded as sci-fi cinema's first feature. Unable to adapt to changing times, he went out of business as a moviemaker around the start of WWI, during which many of his movies were destroyed.

Georges Méliès: Select Filmography

1897: *Le Cabinet de Méphistophélès*
1898: *Le Rêve d'un Astronome*
1899: *Le Miroir de Cagliostro*
1900: *Coppelia: La Poupée Animée*
1902: *L'Homme Mouche*
1902: *Le Voyage dans la Lune*
1902: *Le Voyage de Gulliver à Lilliput et Chez les Géants*
1903: *Faust aux Enfers*
1903: *Le Royaume des Fées*
1904: *Le Sirène*
1904: *Le Voyage à Travers l'Impossible*
1906: *Le Dirigeable Fantastique*
1906: *Le Fantôme d'Alger*

1907: *Deux Cents Milles Lieues sous les Mers*
1907: *Satan en Prison*
1907: *Le Tunnel sous la Manche*
1908: *La Poupée Vivante*
1908: *Le Rêve d'un Fumeur d'Opium*
1910: *Apparitions Fantômatiques*
1910: *Galatée*
1910: *Hydrothérapie Fantastique*
1911: *Les Aventures de Baron de Munchhausen*
1912: *Le Conquête du Pôle*

GEORGE PAL (1908 –1980)

Austria–Hungarian-born US director who worked briefly as an animator in Germany before the Nazis came to power, thereafter working in Europe until moving to the US in 1939. He stamped his initial mark in the US with his Puppetoons, of which he made over forty and for which he received a Special Academy Award in 1943. From 1948 through the mid-1960s he directed several special-effects-laden movies important to sci-fi cinema. Probably his best-known movie is one he produced rather than directed: *The War of the Worlds* (1953).

George Pal: Select Filmography

1934: *Ship of the Ether*
1936: *Sinbad*
1938: *Sky Pirates*
1942: *The Sky Princess*
1958: *tom thumb*
1960: *The Time Machine*
1961: *Atlantis, the Lost Continent*
1962: *The Wonderful World of the Brothers Grimm* (parts)
1964: *7 Faces of Dr. Lao*

RIDLEY SCOTT (b1937)

UK-born US director, a major contributor to sci-fi cinema despite his relevant movies being few in number. He began his directing career in TV, his first work of sci-fi interest being for the BBC series *Adam Adamant Lives!* (1966–7).

Ridley Scott: Select Filmography
1979: *Alien*
1982: *Blade Runner*
1985: *Legend*
2001: *Hannibal*

STEVEN SPIELBERG (b1946)
The most significant moviemaker in recent history. Of his early features, *Duel* (1971) is a cult favourite, but it was with *Jaws* (1975) that he really forced his way to directorial prominence; since then he has never looked back. Many of the movies he has directed, produced, co-produced or executive produced have been in the sci-fi/fantasy genre; the select listing below includes only those he has directed. In 2005 he was reportedly working on a fourth *Indiana Jones* movie. The company he cofounded in 1994, Dreamworks, has likewise been a major contributor to the cinema of the fantastic.

Steven Spielberg: Select Filmography
1964: *Firelight*
1977: *Close Encounters of the Third Kind*
1981: *Raiders of the Lost Ark*
1982: *E.T. – The Extra-Terrestrial*
1983: *Twilight Zone: The Movie* (part)
1984: *Indiana Jones and the Temple of Doom*
1989: *Indiana Jones and the Last Crusade*
1989: *Always*
1991: *Hook*
1993: *Jurassic Park*
1997: *The Lost World: Jurassic Park II*
2001: *A.I.: Artificial Intelligence* (bulk of)
2002: *Minority Report*
2004: *The Terminal*
2005: *War of the Worlds*

ANDREI TARKOVSKY (1932–1986)

One of Russia's greatest directors, even though his filmography is not extensive; he defected to the West a few years before his death. Two of his three major sci-fi movies are very widely known. The third, *Offret* (1986), a reflection on nuclear holocaust, is less seen. To audiences reared on Hollywood, Tarkovsky's movies seem long and static, and his prodigious strengths – notably his extraordinary knack for imbuing small details with powerful resonance – can seem pointless. But his intention was to make movies for grown-ups.

Andrei Tarkovsky: Select Filmography

1972: *Solyaris* (vt *Solaris*)
1979: *Stalker*
1983: *Tempo di viaggio* (TV movie)
1986: *Offret – Sacrificatio*

PAUL VERHOEVEN (b1938)

Dutch-born US director whose European sensibilities have led some to brand him a fringe pornographer – a reputation probably enhanced by his non-sci-fi blockbuster *Basic Instinct* (1992).

Paul Verhoeven: Select Filmography

1987: *RoboCop*
1990: *Total Recall*
1997: *Starship Troopers*
2000: *Hollow Man*

JAMES WHALE (1889–1957)

UK-born US director of horror movies, some of which are sci-fi classics. A practising homosexual at a time when this was frowned upon by US society, he committed suicide by drowning himself in his swimming pool. A fine movie about his last days, *Gods and Monsters* dir Bill Condon, was released in 1998.

James Whale: Select Filmography
1931: *Frankenstein*
1932: *The Old Dark House*
1933: *The Invisible Man*
1935: *Bride of Frankenstein*

EDWARD D. WOOD JR (1924–1978)

US director, renowned both for his appallingly poor writing and directorial skills and for his transvestism: his first marriage ended unconsummated when his bride discovered on their wedding night that he was wearing female underwear. Fittingly, his first movie, *Glen or Glenda* (1953), was about a sex change. By the end of his career he was making porn. Tim Burton made the biopic *Ed Wood* in 1994.

Ed Wood: Select Filmography
1953: *Glen or Glenda*
1955: *Bride of the Monster*
1959: *Night of the Ghouls*
1959: *Plan 9 from Outer Space*
1961: *The Sinister Urge*
1971: *Necromania: A Tale of Weird Love*

ON A HIGHER PLANE: THE CLASSICS OF SCI-FI CINEMA

What is it that makes a sci-fi movie a classic? The parameters differ from those a mainstream cinema critic might use, for such factors as clumsiness of execution do not necessarily disqualify a sci-fi movie from classic status. Rather, some happy combination of plot, core ideas, cleverness, direction, casting, effects and – not least – era can single out a sci-fi movie. Of course, some of sci-fi's great movies are superlative pieces by any standard, and are classics of the cinema as a whole. Others are just tremendous viewing experiences, oft to be repeated.

1902: Le Voyage dans la Lune
(vt *A Trip to the Moon*)
Dir Georges Méliès

Based on elements drawn from Jules Verne's *From the Earth to the Moon* (1865) and H.G. Wells's *First Men in the Moon* (1901), this was sci-fi cinema's first epic, at 21 minutes, and probably Méliès's finest movie. A spaceship is launched to the Moon by a giant cannon, smiting the Man in the Moon smack in the eye. Its crew discover and do battle with the Selenites before escaping back to Earth.

The pirated US version of this movie was retitled, absurdly, *A Trip to Mars*.

1926: **METROPOLIS**
Dir Fritz Lang

Originally released at 182 minutes, but about half has now been lost; the best extant version is probably the 1984 reconstruction by Giorgio Moroder (with rock soundtrack). The supertechnological city Metropolis is built upon an underground city whose machines keep the inhabitants of Metropolis in luxury; even further below is an extensive underground slum, where live the workers who operate the machines. Inventor/alchemist Rotwang creates a robot simulacrum in imitation of and to subvert the efforts of the lovely Maria, who is preaching peace and egalitarianism among the workers. The astonishing power of the direction and of Brigitte Helm's dual performance as Maria and the robot turn what could be a nonsense into a landmark of sci-fi cinema.

1931: **DOCTOR JEKYLL AND MR. HYDE**
Dir Rouben Mamoulian

The first talkie version of RLS's 1886 novella, long lost to obscurity because MGM tried to "disappear" it to make way for their 1941 version starring Spencer Tracy – to which version this is far superior. A blinding performance by Fredric March in the title roles was rewarded with an Oscar.

1931: **FRANKENSTEIN**
Dir James Whale

Bearing many resemblances to Mary Shelley's pivotal 1818 novel, this movie has contributed central elements to Western culture's modern iconography. As a movie it was surpassed by its sequel, *Bride of Frankenstein* (1935), also dir Whale; but it's from this earlier movie that we draw such shared icons as the vengeful mob of villagers, the murderous brain, the mad scientist and his dwarfish servant, and of course the Monster himself.

Mankind's First Fantastic Flight to Venus – the Female Planet!
Queen of Outer Space (1958)

1933: **KING KONG**
Dir Merian C. Cooper and Ernest B. Schoedsack

Like 1931's *Frankenstein*, one of cinema's great contributors to modern iconography. The natives of a remote island worship a giant ape who lives there, Kong. A film crew goes to investigate, and Kong takes a fancy to one visitor, Ann Darrow (Fay Wray). Brought back to New York, the ape panics and is finally shot down by fighter planes from his perch atop the Empire State Building. The special effects by Willis O'Brien were a marvel of their era.

1935: **BRIDE OF FRANKENSTEIN**
Dir James Whale

Frankenstein has abandoned his experiments, but then on the scene arrives Doctor Pretorius, who has learned how to imbue life into the inanimate; he demonstrates (with excellent special effects) using a set of mannequins. Excitedly Frankenstein sets about making a very human-like bride (Elsa Lanchester, in a stunning performance) for his Monster. But she is revolted by the Monster, who runs amok. Even better than its predecessor.

1936: **THINGS TO COME**
Dir William Cameron Menzies

WWII breaks out in 1940 and lasts for decades. In the mid-1960s, the pacifist organization Wings Over the World begins to impose itself, and by 2036 has established a technological utopia. Some rebel against its oversanitization, focusing their wrath on an imminent space shot. Two astronauts – called Adam and Eve! – escape the mob and blast off to find another world. Loosely based on H.G. Wells's *The Shape of Things to Come* (1933), and made with Wells's close involvement, this transcends its trite plot thanks to the awesome sweep of Menzies's direction and in particular his (uncredited) visuals.

1950: **DESTINATION MOON**
Dir Irving Pichel

Based loosely on Robert A. Heinlein's novel *Rocketship Galileo* (1947), and with Heinlein as part of the screenwriting team, this is less a sci-fi movie than a predictive quasi-documentary about humankind's first voyage to the Moon. With a good effort at realism and with astonishing visuals (Chesley Bonestell was Technical Adviser), *Destination Moon* is absorbing to watch, and established a new benchmark toward which future sci-fi movies should strive.

1951: **THE DAY THE EARTH STOOD STILL**
Dir Robert Wise

The rulers of the Galaxy, concerned about humankind's development of the atom bomb, send a humanoid representative, Klaatu, and a gigantic robot, Gort, as emissaries to Earth to tell humanity to give up its bellicose ways or be destroyed. Earth's future is in the balance, but Klaatu discovers how good ordinary people can be, and decrees humankind will be spared ... at least for now. Although suffering a loopholed plot, the movie, with its rallying cry against US militaristic jingoism, is still intensely watchable today.

1951: **THE THING**
Dir Christian Nyby and (uncredited) Howard Hawks

Among the finest monster movies ever made. A flying saucer crashes in the Antarctic, and its sole survivor kills, one by one, the members of the scientific team sent to investigate. Supposedly based on the John W. Campbell Jr (writing as Don A. Stuart) story "Who Goes There?" (1938), this movie omitted Campbell's main plot element: that the alien is a shapeshifter, capable of mimicking team members. This deficit was remedied in the 1982 version, *The Thing* (dir John Carpenter). One of the 1951 version's direct descendants has been *Alien* (1979).

The movie's final line – "Keep watching the skies" – has become immortal.

1953: **THE WAR OF THE WORLDS**
Dir Byron Haskin

The main plot elements of H.G. Wells's 1898 novel transplanted from Victorian England to 1950s California with a surprising degree of cinematic success. The Martians move around in flying craft rather than ambulatory tripods because the special effects for the former were cheaper. Although it is made evident that God's help is pointless, Wells's own fairly argued but eventually dismissive rationalism is replaced by respect for Christian piety. The movie, complete with tacky romantic subplot, became the template for alien-invasion movies.

1956: **FORBIDDEN PLANET**
Dir Fred McLeod Wilcox

Based loosely on Shakespeare's *The Tempest* (c1611), but set on a remote planet. An expedition arrives on Altair IV and finds only two survivors of the previous expedition: Dr Morbius and his daughter Altaira. The long-dead race (the Krel) who once populated this planet died out when their technology permitted them to reify their own worst nightmares; Morbius is well on toward repeating the trick. Worth watching for fabulous scenes amid the Krel's artefacts; pity about Robby the Robot.

1956: **INVASION OF THE BODY SNATCHERS**
Dir Don Siegel

Based on Jack Finney's 1955 novel *The Body Snatchers*, this is the movie *par excellence* of that period in US cinema marked by Cold War paranoia, where (usually) aliens stood in for commies; in this instance the target is arguably less communism than the willing surrender of individuality within US society. Here the aliens are extinguishing folk and taking their places in the guise of exact simulacra who share the alien group mind. Our heroes try to expose and counter the Pod People. An upbeat ending was added at the studio's demand; the original ending suggests we're already becoming Pod People.

1960: THE TIME MACHINE
Dir George Pal

H.G. Wells's 1895 novella filmed for the first time. Here Wells's pessimistic original becomes more of an adventure yarn, but there is great strength in the movie's depiction of the Eloi's and Morlocks' future society.

1961: THE DAY THE EARTH CAUGHT FIRE
Dir Val Guest

High tension is based on a wonderfully improbable quasi-Velikovskian plot: multiple H-bomb tests knock the Earth out of its orbit and spiralling in toward the Sun. Where the movie really scores is in setting much of the action within the editorial office of a newspaper (the *Daily Express*, in fact), so that we experience the compounding catastrophe at second hand, emphasizing our powerlessness to avert it.

1963: THE DAY OF THE TRIFFIDS
Dir Freddie Francis (uncredited) and Steve Sekely

Based on John Wyndham's 1952 novel of the same name, this is at the same time both rather bad and memorably impressive. A meteor storm blinds almost all humanity, leaving them doubly vulnerable to the invasion of Earth by sentient, mobile, homicidal plants.

1964: DR STRANGELOVE, OR
HOW I LEARNED TO STOP WORRYING AND LOVE THE BOMB
Dir Stanley Kubrick

Dark satire based on Peter George's 1958 novel *Two Hours to Doom* (vt *Red Alert*). Apparently Kubrick initially intended to play the story straight, as George's novel did (and as 1964's similarly themed *Fail Safe* did), but wisely opted for humour in telling how human folly, jingoism, stupidity and failure of imagination dance us willingly to nuclear annihilation.

1965: ALPHAVILLE
Jean-Luc Goddard

A surrealistic interplanetary *noir* fantasy featuring Peter Cheyney's tough-guy P.I. Lemmy Caution. One of the true oddities of cinema.

1967: QUATERMASS AND THE PIT
(vt *Five Million Years to Earth*)
Dir Roy Ward Baker

Excavations under a London tube station unearth what proves to be a millions-year-old spaceship from Mars, and the investigators soon begin to be afflicted by horrific psychological and poltergeist manifestations ...

1968: PLANET OF THE APES
Dir Franklin J. Schaffner

Based very loosely on Pierre Boulle's satirical 1963 novel *La planète des singes* (vt *Monkey Planet*). A spaceship unknowingly goes through a time warp to crashland on a far-future Earth where nonhuman apes are the dominant creatures, humans being merely animals. The iconographic sequence is of Charlton Heston discovering the timeworn Statue of Liberty and realizing the hideous truth. There were four movie sequels, two TV series (one animated) and a 2001 remake – all at best undistinguished and the last pretty dire.

1968: 2001: A SPACE ODYSSEY
Dir Stanley Kubrick

Derived ultimately from Arthur C. Clarke's 1951 short story "The Sentinel", and arguably *the* central work of sci-fi cinema. It is composed of three parts: a section where an enigmatic monolith brings intelligence to the pre-human apes of Earth; a long section (the bulk of the movie) set in the near future when humankind discovers the monolith or its duplicate on the Moon and sends an expedition (bedevilled by the increasing insanity of the computer HAL9000) to Jovian orbit and the lunar monolith's counterpart; and a final near-hallucinogenic voyage through space and time as the alien consciousness embraces the surviving crew member. The central section has its longueurs – too many Clarkean self-indulgent digressions to explore the wonders of future technology (ooh, *videophones!*) – but *2001* remains as astonishing an achievement as it ever was.

In the sequel, *2010* (1984), dir Peter Hyams, the aliens ignite Jupiter (in reality an "almost-star") so that its moons become new worlds for humankind to colonize.

1971: A CLOCKWORK ORANGE
Dir Stanley Kubrick

Based on Anthony Burgess's 1962 novel, this was a *cause célèbre* at the time of release because of its supposed glamorization of violence. The concern of the movie is the price we must be prepared to pay if we want to preserve free will. A psychopathic near-future street hooligan undergoes an aversion therapy almost as sadistic as his own behaviour; the therapy is effective, but renders him useless as a member of the society which, like it or not, he inhabits.

1972: SOLYARIS (vt *Solaris*)
Dir Andrei Tarkovsky

Foolishly billed on release in the West as "The Russian *2001*". Long, slow-paced, mood-filled epic, based on the 1961 Stanislaw Lem novel about a living planet that attempts to communicate by altering the perceptions of those who observe it, reifying their wishes. Not a movie for those who like car chases. Visually astonishing, despite somewhat hokey special effects.

Strange Power from Another Planet Menaces the Earth!!
The Day the Earth Stood Still (1951)

1973: SLEEPER
Dir Woody Allen

A 20th-century man awakens from a 200-year deep freeze to find most of the attitudes he embraces have been turned on their heads. Often hilarious, often satirical, sometimes self-indulgent and just plain silly.

1973: SOYLENT GREEN
Dir Richard Fleischer

Based on Harry Harrison's 1966 novel *Make Room! Make Room!*, and regarded by many as a travesty of it. This was Edward G. Robinson's last movie; ironically, his final scene in it has him being rocked tranquilly off to the Final Sleep. In a hideously overpopulated near-future USA, Soylent Green is the newest government-issue foodstuff, its composition a mystery until detective Charlton Heston discovers the awful truth: "Soylent Green is *people!*"

1974: DARK STAR
Dir John Carpenter

Held in such low esteem at the time that it was not released in the UK until 1978, Carpenter's debut, a darkly comic space opera, has become a cult movie.

1977: CLOSE ENCOUNTERS OF THE THIRD KIND
Dir Steven Spielberg

The ultimate UFO movie, and one of the few watchable ones. Like much of ufology, the plot is full of logical holes, but all such considerations are forgotten amid the splendour of the aliens' finally making contact, on their terms, with humankind. The movie, which Spielberg wrote himself, is actually faithful to its material, unlike most UFO-related sci-fi movies. A similar fidelity was shown in the fifteen-hour-long TV miniseries *Taken*, which Spielberg executive-produced in 2002.

1977: **STAR WARS**
Dir George Lucas

The movie which, with *Close Encounters*, did more than any before to banish the last vestiges of the notion that sci-fi movies were mere special-interest fodder: from now on they were regarded as box-office blockbusters. The plot is a fairy tale recast as space opera.

1978: **SUPERMAN – THE MOVIE**
Dir Richard Donner

"You'll Believe a Man Can Fly!" the tagline told us and, although the special effects weren't quite good enough for that, the movie had enough brio that no one minded. *Superman* was a great success, and since then Hollywood has relentlessly brought us more and more comics-superhero adaptations.

1979: **ALIEN**
Dir Ridley Scott

The first in what became a distinguished series. On a remote planet the crew of the spaceship *Nostromo* inadvertently acquire an alien that proves exceptionally antithetical to human life and starts picking them off one by one. Artists involved in the realization included particularly H.R. Giger.

1982: **BLADE RUNNER**
Dir Ridley Scott

Argued by many to be the finest commercial sci-fi movie ever made (despite an artificial upbeat ending grafted on at studio insistence), this was based on Philip K. Dick's 1968 novel *Do Androids Dream of Electric Sheep?* Androids called replicants, built with a predetermined failure date, do the dirty jobs in space for a humankind horrendously overcrowded at home. On occasion replicants can run loose, and blade runners are sent to hunt them down and destroy them. Harrison Ford is one such blade runner; sent after an escaped group of the most sophisticated replicants yet, he finds himself confronted by deep questions about the meaning of humanity. Philip K. Dick posthumously became, for good and for bad, one of Hollywood's hottest properties.

1982: E.T. – THE EXTRATERRESTRIAL
Dir Steven Spielberg

Like *Star Wars* (1977), a sciencefictional fairy tale; one critic at the time remarked that *E.T.* could have been scripted by Peter Pan. Its story – the child alien cast adrift on Earth and sheltered by human children – is now universally known.

1985: BRAZIL
Dir Terry Gilliam

A clerk escapes the miseries of life in a future totalitarian world by imagining himself as a swashbuckling hero. But when an encounter with anarchist rebels draws him into exactly such swashbuckling, he discovers the powers the state possesses to humiliate, torture, isolate and ultimately suppress the individual. Idiosyncratic and eventually powerful.

1986: ALIENS
Dir James Cameron

The sequel to 1979's *Alien* packs considerably more firepower, but often at the expense of atmosphere: more is not necessarily better. Even so, it's an astonishing achievement, and one of the truly great shoot-em-ups of sci-fi cinema.

1989: BACK TO THE FUTURE: PART 2
Dir Robert Zemeckis

The central movie of the *Back to the Future* time-travel trilogy, and the one least liked on release, is darker and as science fiction considerably more sophisticated than its companions.

1991: DELICATESSEN
Dir Marc Caro and Jean-Pierre Jeunet

In a post-holocaust society, food is currency and meat the most valued currency of all. A young ex-clown discovers his prospective father-in-law intends to make him a source of "special cuts" ... This French movie offers the darkest of dark comedies.

1991: TERMINATOR 2: JUDGEMENT DAY
Dir James Cameron

Like Cameron's 1986 *Aliens*, a sequel that commands greater firepower than the original (*The Terminator*, 1984) – but this time to far better effect, since the pyrotechnics are matched by a thoughtful and often cautionary script: try as we might to project our own viciousness onto the machines we create, it's not the machines that are the true terminators, but us.

1992: ALIEN³
Dir David Fincher

Perhaps the best of the *Alien* series, although coolly received on release and with some clunky special effects. In a grimily realized penal colony, the vile machinations of The Company – the covert organization intent on utilizing the aliens as weapons of control – are slowly disclosed, and its principals are seen to be more evil than either the alien or the colony's sex-murderers.

1992: ORLANDO
Dir Sally Potter

Based on the 1928 Virginia Woolf novel, this recounts episodes in the life of a gender-variable immortal. An important subtext is the inconsequentiality of the physical frame beside the true element of identity: the self. "Same person," murmurs the Orlando on finding herself this time a woman. "No difference at all – just a different sex."

1993: **BODY SNATCHERS**
Dir Abel Ferrara

A revisualization of the story earlier filmed in 1956 and 1978, this time as a thinking person's thriller set on a military base where the daughter of one of the science personnel finds her alienation from those around her has to do with more than adolescence. Bizarrely, in the UK this top-notch movie was relegated to direct-to-video release.

1994: **STARGATE**
Dir Roland Emmerich

A mixture of fantasy, pulp sf and Indiana Jones. An ancient artefact offers a gateway to distant planets. The human team sent through it discovers an ancient-Egypt-style civilization tyrannized by an alien, who is the god Osiris. Splendidly realized, this has spawned a number of highly successful TV series.

1996: **INDEPENDENCE DAY**
Dir Roland Emmerich

Aliens invade and prepare to exterminate humanity. Plucky Americans triumph over enormous odds. Jingoistic garbage, yes, but *glorious* jingoistic garbage.

1996: 12 MONKEYS
Dir Terry Gilliam

Elaborate time-travel tale based loosely on the 1962 French short *La Jetée*, written by and dir Chris Marker. In 1996 a virus, supposedly spread by a terrorist group called The Army of the 12 Monkeys, virtually wiped out humankind. The people of 2035 send a man back in time to 1996 in an attempt to avert the disaster. Unfortunately he overshoots, arriving in 1990, and, as he tries to explain himself, is locked up in a mental institution, powerless to forestall the tragedy.

1997: CONTACT
Dir Robert Zemeckis

Based on the 1985 novel by Carl Sagan. A young SETI scientist discovers radio signals from an extraterrestrial civilization, which she deciphers as the instructions for building a complex machine (as in the 1961 BBC TV serial *A for Andromeda* written by Fred Hoyle and John Elliot). Through its use she undergoes a hallucinatory trip among the beings of the cosmos. The movie questions whether there can indeed be any common ground between scientific rationalism and religious faith.

1997: DARK CITY
Dir Alex Proyas

In a city where it is always night, a man wakens without memory and finds he is wanted for a string of murders. Fugitive, he uncovers more and more perplexities about the always-dark city, including the presence of The Strangers, who can remould reality around them. How much is real and how much is within his own mind, and is there any difference? An enormous cult success.

1997: THE FIFTH ELEMENT
Dir Luc Besson

A quirky and chaotic futuristic piece, mixing much brilliance with much self-indulgence; at its best, however, it shines more brightly than a score of most other sci-fi movies put together ... as one might expect from Besson. Every 5000 years Evil tries to swamp our world; only through utilization of the fifth element, which proves to be an enigmatic young woman, can Evil's aims – and the aims of evil humans – be thwarted.

1997: GATTACA
Dir Andrew Niccol

In a future world, only the genetically perfect can succeed. Vincent dreams of being an astronaut, but has a genetic disposition for heart failure. With the aid of a crippled athlete, he fakes his genetic records and rises to prominence within the Gattaca Corporation, whose business is spaceflight. Niccol keeps events carefully understated throughout, rendering his inherently implausible tale surprisingly moving.

1997: THE POSTMAN
Dir Kevin Costner

Perhaps more maligned than any other sf movie, this long post-Holocaust tale (based on the 1985 David Brin novella) shows the scattered remnant of the US population being mustered back toward civilization through the re-establishment of the US Mail. Critics slam the length and implausibilities; others find it engrossing and hail the power of its mythopoeia (of which latter the implausibilities are part).

1999: THE MATRIX
Dir Andy and Larry Wachowski

A movie that caught the *Zeitgeist*, relying heavily on the works of cyberpunk authors like William Gibson, on cinematic precursors like Terry Gilliam's *12 Monkeys* (1996), and on Asian martial arts movies. A hacker believes he is living in the late 20th century but discovers he is imprisoned in an illusion created two centuries later by the machine that controls, and essentially is, the world.

2000: A BEAUTIFUL MIND
Dir Ron Howard

A biography told almost entirely through his delusions of mathematical genius John Nash, a schizophrenic. Astonishingly beautiful, chilling and powerful, with a first-rate performance from Russell Crowe as Nash, the movie won four Oscars™ (including Best Director and Best Picture, but bizarrely not Best Actor) and a host of other awards.

2002: 28 DAYS LATER . . .
Dir Danny Boyle

A month after a plague has turned most of the UK population into zombies, the few who're uninfected, even as their numbers dwindle, survive as best they can. The post-holocaust movie pared down to its essentials and (despite obvious implausibility) all the grimmer for that.

2004: THE DAY AFTER TOMORROW
Dir Roland Emmerich

Although derided by critics on scientific grounds, this movie nonetheless displayed a better understanding of climate science than did the contemporary US Government. Global warming triggers the astonishingly rapid advent of an ice age. Attempts to protect against the worst effects of the disaster are thwarted by the stupidity of the US Vice-President, who ignores all warnings for "economic" reasons. In bizarre irony, all of the TV reports shown in the movie are from Rupert Murdoch affiliates, mainly Fox News, the US news service that in real life does most to pooh-pooh warnings about climate change.

2004: ETERNAL SUNSHINE OF THE SPOTLESS MIND
Dir Michel Gondry

A doctor has devised a technique of selectively erasing memories. When Clementine eliminates all memory of her lover Joel, he seeks solace from his grief by having his memories of Clementine eradicated. But the process does not go smoothly, and the two engage in a flight through crumbling and artificial memories as they journey to rediscover each other.

Buck Rogers Battles Invasion from Foreign Planets! Space Ships Exploded by Giant Ray Machines! Mountains Crumbled by Disintegrating Machines!
Buck Rogers (1939)

They Created a Monster Over Lunch. Now It's Back for Dinner . . .
Deep Space (1987)

See the Monster Beat a Man to Death with His Own Arm
The Monster and the Stripper (1968)

The Most Legendary Monster of All Can Now Be Seen for the First Time!
The Watcher in the Woods (1980)

You Scream! You Expand! You Explode! A New Source of Evil is Discovered and is Out of Control.
Spasms (1983)

Same Planet. New Scum.
Men in Black II (2002)

The Bavarian Answer to Planet of the Apes!
Space Zoo (2001)

Two Mortals Trapped in Outer Space, Challenging the Unearthly Furies of an Outlaw Planet Gone Mad!!
This Island Earth (1955)

SCARING YOUR PANTS OFF: SCI-FI MEETS SEX

There are countless soft-porn (and a few hard-porn) sci-fi movies around, most being direct-to-video productions characterized by brief moments of bad sf interspersed by long slo-mo scenes of simulated sex and drearily repetitive music; the seven episodes (so far) of *Emmanuelle in Space* are typical. But some mainstream sci-fi movies have confronted the subject of sex forthrightly, for satirical, serious or exploitational reasons.

1949: THE PERFECT WOMAN
Dir Bernard Knowles

An inventor makes a female android and, to test its realism, hires a man to take it out on a date. However, the inventor's niece, whom he used as his model for the android, in a spirit of mischief substitutes herself. What follows is predictable to anyone familiar with British sex comedies: much fancy underwear.

1967: BARBARELLA
Dir Roger Vadim

A glossy exploitation movie. With Terry Southern among an army of eight credited screenwriters, one expects a comic satirical edge to this interplanetary sex fantasia, and sure enough it's there in this screen adaptation of Jean-Claude Forest's comic strip.

Unfortunately, script, cast (notably Jane Fonda and Milo O'Shea) and crew are significantly better than Vadim's direction, which seems to think all the rest is just window-dressing for Fonda's skin.

1968: **THE YEAR OF THE SEX OLYMPICS**
Dir Michael Elliott

Scripted by Nigel Kneale, this bitter satire depicts a future in which people are so controlled, largely by mind-numbing TV, that they no longer feel anything very much – not lust, not anger, not hate, not love. Even the imminent televising of the sex olympics attracts only mild interest.

1974: **FLESH GORDON**
Dir Michael Benveniste

It began as just another piece of porn, its title and plot being – as so often with such movies – in parody of a better-known movie. However, various of Hollywood's special-effects wizards heard about it and volunteered their services; the budget was greatly increased and the sex toned down for mainstream audiences. The resulting box-office success can be seen as one of the inspirations for *Flash Gordon* (1980), dir Michael Hodges. The sequel was *Flesh Gordon II* (1991), dir Howard Ziehm.

1974: **SHIVERS**
(vt *The Parasite Murders*, vt *They Came from Within*)
Dir David Cronenberg

A doctor creates phallic parasites that have the properties of both an aphrodisiac and an STD. The effects of casual promiscuity are gorily reified.

Beauties! The Prey of a Monster's Desires!
Lycanthropus (1962)

1976: **RABID**
Dir David Cronenberg

A medical operation inadvertently turns a woman (played by porn star Marilyn Chambers) into a blood-lusting killer who starts an epidemic of such killers, spreading the disease via a phallic syringe that appears under the arm.

1976: **THE MAN WHO FELL TO EARTH**
Dir Nicolas Roeg

An alien arrives secretly on Earth planning to accelerate human technological ability and simultaneously build a fortune so he may rescue his family from their dying planet. Slowly, however, he is emotionally, psychologically and sexually corrupted by those around him until reduced at last to the status of a mere human, suffering the human condition: great dreams that he will never be able to realize.

1982: **VIDEODROME**
Dir David Cronenberg

An unscrupulous cable-TV boss will distribute anything so long as it makes money. He discovers the obscure rogue Videodrome channel, whose "programmes" comprise horrific sexual torture and murder; are the depicted scenes staged or real? Fascinated, he is drawn by the lure of this taboo sexuality into the media fringe where reality and the imaginary are indistinguishable.

1988: **EARTH GIRLS ARE EASY**
Dir Julien Temple

Three hairy alien males crashland in San Fernando Valley, California, and, once given a bodily shave, are sufficiently humanoid to be mobbed by babes. This bizarre, shambolic musical comedy, in which Valley culture is portrayed as more alien than the aliens' own, may not be very good but has a high degree of . . . lovability.

1988: MY STEPMOTHER IS AN ALIEN
Dir Richard Benjamin

Dire, startlingly unfunny sex comedy in which an alien race, desperate to save itself from extinction, sends one of its number in the guise of a fabulously sexy woman to boff a witless astronomer into sending an energy beam that will be the salvation of their species ...

1995: SPECIES
Dir Roger Donaldson

SETI observers receive instructions for creating alien DNA (shades of the 1961 BBC TV serial *A for Andromeda* written by Fred Hoyle and John Elliot) and splicing it into human DNA. The result is a sensual woman who can shapeshift at will into a near-invulnerable killing creature. She uses her sexuality to lure victims – and of course must be stopped before she has a chance to breed.

In the first sequel, *Species II* (1998) dir Peter Medak, an astronaut returns from Mars possessed by an alien and mutates into a sex-mad monster. The second, direct-to-video sequel, *Species III* (2004) dir Brad Turner, essentially reprises the first movie.

1999: THE ASTRONAUT'S WIFE
Dir Rand Ravich

Two NASA shuttle astronauts inexplicably lose contact with Mission Control for a couple of minutes, but all seems well after the interruption. On their return to Earth they're outwardly normal, but the wife of one, observing the many changes in his behaviour – not least in bed – slowly realizes he's an alien counterfeit. And she becomes pregnant by him ...

The Story of a Guy, a Girl and an Alien –
and One Night They Will Always Remember!
Voyage of the Rock Aliens (1988)

2001: THE WOMAN EVERY MAN WANTS
Dir Gabriela Tagliavini

US/Argentine movie depicting a futuristic society which females dominate. Intimidated by all these dominant women, a man buys an android woman as his social and sexual companion, and falls in love with it/her.

2002: S1M0NE
Dir Andrew Niccol

A washed-up movie director, tired of actors' tantrums, creates a virtual woman using a sophisticated computer program, and stars her in his next movie. The world falls in love with her and refuses to believe she is anything other than a real (and perfect) woman. A satire on the one hand of religious belief but also of the mass tendency to respond sexually toward images rather than real people.

2002: TEKNOLUST
Dir Lynn Hershman-Leeson

Surrealist caper starring Tilda Swinton as cyber-geneticist Rosetta Stone and as the three Self-Replicating Automata she creates from her own DNA. The SRAs are capable of escaping the computer software in which they are normally bound. In the outside world they seduce men to gain the male chromosomes they require for survival, but in so doing they spread a mysterious STD.

To Save His Planet, an Alien Must Find a Woman on Earth to Have His Baby. There's Just One Problem . . .
What Planet Are You From? (2000)

Screaming Young Girls Sucked into a Labyrinth of Horror by a Blood-Starved Ghoul from Hell!!
Beast from Haunted Cave (1959)

THE ILLUSION OF LIFEFORMS: ANIMATED SCI-FI

Of course, most modern sci-fi movies are, strictly speaking, in large part animated, insofar as their special effects rely heavily on CGI and sometimes on stop-motion and even traditional animation. But there's a distinction between live-action movies that contain a great deal of animated special effects, on the one hand, and animated movies (including live-action/animated movies), on the other: the *intent*. In the former type of movie, the purpose of the animation is to deceive the viewer into believing s/he is watching something real. In the latter, not only is there no pretence the animation is anything other than what it is, the fact that the movie is in whole or in part animated is a primary element of its appeal.

Here we look at some representatives of the long and distinguished history of animated sci-fi movies.

c1921: **THE FLYING HOUSE**
Dir Winsor McCay

One of McCay's three *Dreams of the Rarebit Fiend* animated shorts. A wife dreams the house is threatened with repossession and that her husband fits it with wings, so they can fly off in search of somewhere the mortgage company will never find them. A storm sweeps them to the Moon, but they are repulsed by the Man in the Moon. Jolted out of space by a close encounter with a rocket, they find themselves safely back in bed.

1941: SUPERMAN
Dir Dave Fleischer

First of a series of 17 nine-minute animated shorts produced by the Fleischers and released between 1941 and 1943. Nominated for an Oscar, this first outing has Superman dealing with an archetypal Mad Scientist and his "electrothanasia ray". The series is as follows (with directors noted when not Dave Fleischer):

1941 *1: Superman* (vt *The Mad Scientist*)
1941 *2: The Mechanical Monsters*
1942 *3: Billion Dollar Limited*
1942 *4: The Arctic Giant*
1942 *5: The Bulleteers*
1942 *6: The Magnetic Telescope*
1942 *7: Electric Earthquake*
1942 *8: Volcano*
1942 *9: Terror on the Midway*
1942 *10: Japoteurs*, dir Seymour Kneitel
1942 *11: Showdown*, dir Isidore Sparber
1942 *12: Eleventh Hour*, dir Dan Gordon
1942 *13: Destruction, Inc.*, dir Isidore Sparber
1943 *14: The Mummy Strikes*, dir Isidore Sparber
1943 *15: Jungle Drums*, dir Dan Gordon
1943 *16: Underground World*, dir Seymour Kneitel
1943 *17: Secret Agent*, dir Seymour Kneitel

1953: DUCK DODGERS IN THE 24TH CENTURY
Dir Chuck Jones

A seven-minute parody of the Buck Rogers cycle; introduced Marvin the Martian to we inferior beings.

1973: LA PLANÈTE SAUVAGE (vt *Fantastic Planet*)
Dir René Laloux

Based on Stefan Wul's novel *Oms en série* (1957). Long ago, humans destroyed their own world; now they live as Oms – pets or pests of the gigantic humanoid Draags – on the planet Yagam. The Oms capture a spaceship and journey to Yagam's moon, the Fantastic Planet, which they discover is where the Draags' souls go to engage in a sort of spiritual reproduction with the souls of beings from other worlds.

1977: **WIZARDS**
Dir Ralph Bakshi

Set two million years after a holocaust has largely destroyed the world, this depicts a new war between Good and Evil. Amid all the trappings of Nazi Germany, an evil wizard attempts to launch another holocaust but is matched by his good-wizard twin brother.

1982: **LES MAÎTRES DU TEMPS** (vt *Time Masters*)
Dir René Laloux

Based on the Stefan Wul novel *L'orphelin de Perdide* (1958) but, more directly, on the comic-book adaptation of it by Moebius as *Les maîtres du temps* (1978). A boy is stranded on the dangerous planet Perdide. The rescuers discover that the servants of an alien species called the Masters of Time are preparing to throw Perdide back in time in order to colonize it at an earlier stage of its existence.

1984: **NAUSICAÄ**
Dir Hayao Miyazaki

Long after a holocaust, humanity clings to existence, mainly as scattered tribes, in the face of an environment dominated by hostile plants and animals. Princess Kushana raises an army to try to conquer the world – in the full sense of that term. The girl Nausicaä, who can communicate at an essential level with the wildlife, realizes cooperation with the environment, not attempted conquest of it, is the way to restore humankind.

1984: **LENSMAN** (vt *Lensman: Secret of the Lens*)
Dir Kazuyuki Hirokawa and Yoshiaki Kawajiri
Based loosely on the novels by E.E. "Doc" Smith. Young Kimball
Kinnison is given the Lens by the dying survivor of a derelict
spacecraft, and must save the Galaxy. It was followed by a 1987–9
TV series and by *Lensman: Power of the Lens* (2000).

1986: **WHEN THE WIND BLOWS**
Dir Jimmy T. Murakami
Based on the 1982 graphic novel by Raymond Briggs, who also
wrote the screenplay, this anti-nukes movie depicts the buildup to
holocaust through the experience of a single working-class
couple as they struggle to make sense of what's going on.

1986: **LAPUTA: CASTLE IN THE SKY** (vt *Castle in the Sky*)
Dir Hayao Miyazaki
Long ago, flying islands tyrannized the groundling nations from on
high; it is believed they were all destroyed, but legend insists that
one, Laputa, is still aloft. Two orphans, aided by a gang of aerial
pirates, reach Laputa – whose huge war robots have now turned
to the peaceful tending of the island's gardens – and free the
island from humanity's lust for power.
*   Originally called *Tenku no Shiro Rapyuta* (vt *Tenku no Shiro
    Laputa*), this saw the substitution of its subtitle for its main
    title in the US market, where salespeople were concerned
    Hispanic parents might be put off: in Spanish "*la puta*"
    means "the whore". What those sensitive Hispanic buyers
    do when their kids encounter *Gulliver's Travels* in school is
    anyone's guess.

1987: **AKIRA**
Dir Katsuhiro Otomo
After the near-destruction of 21st-century Tokyo by the Akira
Project – a military-inspired machine that is part nuclear bomb,
part supercomputer, part god – street hooligans with psychic

powers must tame the monster. The first piece of *anime* to have a major impact on mainstream culture in the West.

1988: GANDAHAR: LES ANNÉES LUMIÈRES
Dir René Laloux

Based on the novel *Les hommes-machines contre Gandahar* (1969) by Jean-Pierre Andrevon. The guards of Gandahar's borders are being killed off. Investigators find that an entity called Métamorphe, based a thousand years in the future, has sent a robot army to turn the planet's inhabitants into stone and transport them to Métamorphe's own time. The younger Métamorphe that exists in the present is enlisted to help counter the actions of its future counterpart.

* The English-language version of this, *Light Years*, was hideously re-edited, with a new script commissioned from Isaac Asimov.

1988: WHO FRAMED ROGER RABBIT
Dir Robert Zemeckis

In an alternate world, Toons have as much reality as human beings but are largely confined to the ghetto of Toontown. A disillusioned P.I. must solve a murder mystery involving humans, Toons, prejudice and corruption. A truly astonishing blend of live action with animation, achieved thanks to the genius of master animator Richard Williams.

* The title is correct without the seemingly obligatory question mark. There's an old and somewhat obscure superstition that a question mark in a movie's title spells box-office disaster, and the studios chose to observe it.

1990: KIDÔ KEISATSU PATOREBÂ: THE MOVIE
(vt *Patlabor: The Movie*, vt *Mobile Police Patlabor*,
vt *PatLabor: The Mobile Police*)
Dir Mamoru Oshii

As a typhoon heads toward future Tokyo, a software virus is making the robots turn rogue. The police and their giant humanoid robots (Labors) are called in to normalize the situation, solve the crime and catch the criminal. Sci-fi meets the tough-guy police procedural.

The sequels so far have been: *Kidô Keisatsu Patorebâ: The Movie 2* (1993; vt *Patlabor: The Movie 2*), dir Oshii, in which the cops must deal with politics, terrorism and martial law; and *WXIII: Patlabor the Movie 3* (2002), dir Takuji Endo and Fumihiko Takayama, in which again terrorists are at work. The latter precedes the former in terms of plot.

1990: JETSONS: THE MOVIE
Dir William Hanna and Joseph Barbera

One of many Hanna–Barbera productions of sci-fi relevance ("interest" would be too strong a word). George Jetson investigates persistent sabotage at an asteroid-mining operation. The saboteurs prove to be cuddly Ewok-style aliens who're trying to save their underground civilization from destruction by the mining operation.

1992: COOL WORLD
Dir Ralph Bakshi

A sophisticated alternative-reality tale. The Cool World has been created by comics artist Jack Deebs as setting for his successful series; however, it also has a reality in parallel with our own world. In the course of an extremely complex plot, Deebs must save our world from invasion by his own creations.

1995: KÔKAKU KIDÔTAI (vt *Ghost in the Shell*)
Dir Mamoru Oshii

In 2029 the real world and the cyberworld are intricately intertwined. Cybercrime is rampant, and so Section Nine is formed, its members cyborgs who can operate with equal effectiveness in both worlds. A Section Nine officer has come to question her own humanity. Elsewhere, a sophisticated piece of commercial sentient software has likewise come to question its status. When the two are brought together, will a new form of life emerge?

This was sequelled by *Inosensu: Kôkaku Kidôtai* (2004; vt *Ghost in the Shell 2: Innocence*), also dir Oshii, set a few years later. A cyborg called Batô struggles to retain his humanity in a world where most humans have given up on such ideas.

1999: THE IRON GIANT
Dir Brad Bird

Based on the 1968 story "The Iron Man" by Ted Hughes. A vast alien robot crashlands in Maine and is befriended by a small boy. However, the robot's size and outward appearance terrify the adult population, and the military step in to destroy the machine. Before they can do so, it demonstrates its moral superiority to the bigots and the bureaucrats by being prepared to sacrifice itself in defence of others.

2000: TITAN A.E.
Dir Don Bluth

A space opera in the same vein as *Star Wars* (1977). The alien Drej destroy the Earth, leaving only a few surviving humans. The youth Cale, whose father has succeeded in hiding a worldship called *Titan* somewhere in the Galaxy, must fight off the Drej and locate *Titan* before they do; when he does, the worldship "unfolds" to become a fresh home for humanity.

2001: METOROPORISU (vt *Metropolis*)
Dir Rintaro

This bears some similarities with Fritz Lang's 1926 classic *Metropolis*, which it seems to have taken as a sparking-off point. In a future society, robots are essentially a slave species confined to the underground levels of a great city, but some are fighting back against the human tyrants.

2001: FINAL FANTASY: THE SPIRITS WITHIN
Dir Hironobu Sakaguchi and Moto Sakakibara

Featuring brilliant CGI animation and many moments of great beauty, this cyberpunk-flavored movie, based on a video game, depicts plucky Earthlings endeavouring in AD2065 to repel alien destruction.

2001: COWBOY BEBOP: TENGOKU NO TOBIRA
(vt *Cowboy Bebop: The Movie*,
vt *Cowboy Bebop: Knockin' On Heavens Door*)
Dir Shinichirô Watanabe

Based on the 1998 future-noir TV series, this sees the Bebop crew of wrong-righters hot on the trail of the cause of a deadly viral plague having been released into the atmosphere. Alarmingly, the criminal responsible seems to be a man who's been dead these past ten years ...

2002: TREASURE PLANET
Dir Ron Clements and John Musker

Based on Robert Louis Stevenson's 1883 novel *Treasure Island*, this translates the story rather limply into interplanetary guise.

2002: LILO & STITCH
Dir Dean DeBlois and Chris Sanders

Aliens develop an aggressive, indestructible creature, which escapes and crashes down on Hawaii, where it is adopted by the adolescent girl Lilo, who adopts it as a pet, calling it Stitch and educating it into sociability. A minor but surprisingly enjoyable movie.

2003: KAENA: LA PROPHÉTIE (vt *Kaena: The Prophecy*)
Dir Chris Delaporte and Pascal Pinon

Within a huge plant called AXIS is a village whose people depend upon the plant and its sap for all they have. However, AXIS is dying, and not all the prayers of the priesthood can ease the rate at which its sap is drying up. The girl Kaena rebels against authority to try to solve the crisis, and in so doing discovers the truth about AXIS – that beneath it lies a whole new world to populate.

2004: SKY CAPTAIN AND THE WORLD OF TOMORROW
Dir Kerry Conran

In most live-action/animated movies, the characters (or some of them) are animated within a live-action world. *Sky Captain* – like much of 1990's *Dick Tracy*, dir Warren Beatty, but to far greater effect – turns this on its head: live actors move within an almost entirely animated world. Further, the images of the actors are processed to make them resemble CGI animations. In an alternate past, 1940s Manhattan is invaded by giant robots. Call for Sky Captain, leader of a private aerial army ... The plot is in homage to pulp adventure fiction of the era; the realization is surpassingly beautiful.

2004: THE INCREDIBLES
Dir Brad Bird

Superhero parents are brought out of retirement, supposedly by the US Government but in fact by a mad inventor who seeks to become the world's greatest-ever superhero. With their three kids, also possessed of superpowers, Mr Incredible and Elastigirl (Mrs Incredible) plus their superhero pal Frozone must confront the villain. The usual excellent CGI animation from Pixar and a script that demonstrates genuine understanding of the superhero genre.

2005: ROBOTS
Dir Chris Wedge and Carlos Saldanha

Set in a world populated entirely by robots, this follows the adventures of a young robot genius inventor who seeks to make his world a better place.

RETURN OF THE LIVING REMAKE

Sometimes it seems as if all Hollywood knows how to produce is remakes, and in no genre is this more true than sci-fi. Here are some of the most-remade stories, plus a few noteworthy remakes.

ALRAUNE

Such was the popularity of Hans Heinz Ewers's 1911 novel that it was filmed at least five times between 1918 and 1952, including twice in 1918 alone. A mad scientist gathers the fresh semen from beneath a hanged sex criminal and impregnates a prostitute with it. The resulting child grows up to be a beautiful young woman incapable of love, named Alraune. (In German the name refers to the supposedly human-shaped mandrake root, which according to legend develops only under the gallows, forming from the semen men eject as they're hanged.) However, her origins cannot remain forever hidden, and she enacts a terrible revenge ...

- Copies of Ewers's novel *Alraune* were distributed to German soldiers during WWII, presumably because it reinforced the racist belief that evil is genetic. He was also the author of the Horst Wessel Song.
- The first 1918 version, made in Germany, was dir Eugen Illes and has been lost.
- The second 1918 version, likewise lost, was an Austrian/Hungarian production dir Mihaly Kertesz (better known later as Michael Curtiz) and Fritz Odon. It differs

from the others in that Alraune is born from a union between a prostitute and a mandrake root. The mind boggles.

- The status of 1919's *Alraune und der Golem* is uncertain. Nothing is known of it beyond a single poster, and it's possible the movie was never made.
- Also released as *Daughter of Destiny* and *Unholy Love*, the 1928 German production was dir Henrik Galeen and starred Brigitte Helm (best known in sci-fi movies as Maria/The Robot in Fritz Lang's 1926 *Metropolis*).
- Another German production starring Brigitte Helm, the 1930 version (vt *Daughter of Evil*) dir Richard Oswald aimed for pedestrian realism, and achieved it.
- Much later came the 1952 West German remake (vt *Mandragore*, vt *Unnatural*, vt *Vengeance*), dir Arthur Maria Rabenalt – better known for his Nazi propaganda movies. With Hildegard Knef as Alraune, this clumsily attempts to reinstate the sensuality and atmosphere of sexual obsession present in the 1928 remake but missing from the 1930 version.

ATTACK OF THE 50 FOOT WOMAN

Made in 1958, the original, dir Nathan Hertz and starring Allison Hayes, was a prime piece of cheesy, low-budget drive-in fodder. A visiting alien tampers with a woman's genes so that she starts growing and growing . . . and becoming gradually more psychotic.

- The 1994 remake, *Attack of the 50 Ft. Woman*, was originally made for HBO but outside the US was released theatrically; it was dir Christopher Guest and starred Daryl Hannah. Not quite an homage, not quite a parody, not quite a straight remake, it ended up being really not quite a movie.

THE BLOB

It's hard to understand the attraction of the original movie *The Blob* (1958), dir Irvin S. Yeaworth Jr, aside from the presence of the young Steve McQueen: the direction is uninspired and the plot (an alien blob of protoplasm devours people until stopped by a bunch of teenage Rebels Without a Clue) is silly. However, it inspired a disastrous late sequel – *Beware! The Blob* (1971), dir Larry Hagman – and a 1988 remake, dir Chuck Russell. This latter has little *raison d'être* except to show off how much special effects had improved over thirty years.

✧

BRIDE OF FRANKENSTEIN

The sequel to the enormously successful *Frankenstein* (1931), dir James Whale, was surprisingly unhurried: *Bride of Frankenstein*, again dir Whale, was not released until 1935; it is the archetypal example of a sequel being even better than its original. Elsa Lanchester turned in a wonderful performance as the Bride to Boris Karloff's Monster.

* In 1973 the UK miniseries (and derived movie) *Frankenstein: The True Story*, dir Jack Smight, reprised many of the elements of the story. Jane Seymour was Prima, the Bride.
* The full-scale remake was *The Bride* (1985), dir Frank Roddam. Regarded as one of sci-fi cinema's great stinkers (see page 82), it had Clancy Brown as the Monster.
* *Bride of Re-Animator* (1990), dir Brian Yuzna, can be read as a skewed parody of the Bride's story.

✧

A CONNECTICUT YANKEE IN KING ARTHUR'S COURT

Numerous movies have been based on Mark Twain's 1889 novel *A Connecticut Yankee in King Arthur's Court*, and this is certainly not a definitive listing. There have also been several animated TV half-hour features, the most enjoyable of which is the 1978 Bugs Bunny vehicle *A Connecticut Rabbit in King Arthur's Court* (vt *Bugs Bunny in King Arthur's Court*).

* Little is known about the 1920 US silent version starring Harry Myers except that it was probably a vehicle for contemporary political satire.
* The 1931 remake was dir David Butler and starred Will

Rogers as the temporal misfit. Timeslipping back to Camelot, he is accused of being a warlock but is able to escape death through his superior knowledge. Again, much sport is made of topical politics.

- The 1949 US musical remake, dir Tay Garnett, was a Bing Crosby vehicle and, though it reverted to the original text, failed to maintain Twain's original, satirical intent: blandness was the key.

- The 1970 US animated TV movie dir Walter J. Hucker has a witty script and animation that veers between humdrum and excellent.

- In 1979 Disney recast the tale as *The Spaceman and King Arthur* (vt *Unidentified Flying Oddball*), dir Russ Mayberry. A truly dreadful movie, but there have been worse adaptations of the tale . . .

- A long (164 minutes) USSR remake, fairly faithful to Twain, was *Novye Priklyucheniya Yanki pri Dvore Korolya Artura: Fantaziya na Temu Marka Tvena*, dir Viktor Gres.

- In the 1989 TV remake, dir Mel Damski, the unconscious temponaut is a 12-year-old black girl (Keshia Knight Pulliam), who brings with her enough gadgetry to establish her value to Arthur's court; rock music and dance play their part. What could have been a ghastly low-budget exercise is more than redeemed by a first-rate script, good direction, and Pulliam's performance.

- The Canadian/Czech/French 1995 remake *A Young Connecticut Yankee in King Arthur's Court* sees another rock-loving youngster transported back in time. Despite a grating disrespect for the Matter of Britain, which succumbs to teenage smartassery, this movie is not as bad as it sounds.

- Also from 1995, the US/UK/Hungarian coproduction *A Kid in King Arthur's Court*, dir Michael Gottlieb, *was* as bad as it sounds. The tagline was: "Joust Do It!"

- The 1998 US TV movie *A Knight in Camelot*, dir Roger Young, sees computer nerd Whoopi Goldberg hoisted back in time, complete with her laptop. Another dud.

- And yet another dud, though not quite so disastrous: the US movie *Black Knight* (2001), dir Gil Junger, sees Martin

Lawrence as an amusement-park employee thrown back to 14th-century England (not King Arthur's court, but the principle's the same). The comedy is lukewarm, but interest is enlivened by the presence of Marsha Thomason.

DOCTOR JEKYLL AND MR HYDE

Stevenson's 1886 novella and the play based upon it by Thomas R. Sullivan have between them provided the basis for countless movies. What follows is a very incomplete list.

- The 1920 US movie *Dr Jekyll and Mr Hyde* was dir John S. Robertson and starred John Barrymore in the title role.
- The next version of note is probably the best of all: *Doctor Jekyll and Mister Hyde*, directed in 1931 by Rouben Mamoulian and starring Fredric March in the title role. March justifiably received an Academy Award.
- Dir Victor Fleming, the 1941 *Dr Jekyll and Mr Hyde* starred Spencer Tracy. Although quite closely based on its predecessor, it's a classic example of "more is less"; e.g., the inclusion of major star Ingrid Bergman as Cockney good-time girl Ivy, a role for which she was overwhelmingly unsuitable.
- *El Hombre y la Bestia* (vt *El Extraño Caso del Hombre y la Bestia*; vt *El Sensacional y Extraño Caso del Hombre y la Bestia*; vt *The Man and the Beast*; vt *The Strange Case of the Man and the Beast*) was an Argentinian offering, dir Mario Soffici and with Soffici himself in the dual role. There was also a Mexican remake with this title, dir Julian Soler and starring Enrique Lizalde, in 1973.
- Seymour Friedman directed the routine Hollywood horror outing *Son of Dr Jekyll* in 1951, with Louis Hayward as a son who finds more than you might expect in his genes.
- And what else would you expect next? *Daughter of Dr Jekyll* (1957), dir Edgar G. Ulmer, had Gloria Talbott accused of being a werewolf because of her paternity.
- In the updated 1959 UK version *The Ugly Duckling* (1959), dir Lance Comfort, Jekyll's respectable descendant Bernard Bresslaw periodically transforms into a teddy boy.
- Hammer Studios got in on the act in 1960 with *The Two Faces*

of Dr Jekyll (vt House of Fright; vt Jekyll's Inferno), dir Terence
Fisher. Paul Massie is Jekyll/Hyde.

- Dir and starring Jerry Lewis, 1963's The Nutty Professor
  reworked the tale in contemporary terms. Rumour has it
  that Buddy Love, the obnoxious Hyde equivalent, was
  modelled on Dean Martin, whose long-time partnership with
  Lewis had recently dissolved.
- The 1968 Canadian/US TV movie Doctor Jekyll and Mister
  Hyde (vt The Strange Case of Doctor Jekyll and Mister Hyde), dir
  Charles Jarrot and starring Jack Palance in the dual role, was
  earnestly faithful.
- Stephen Weeks directed the 1971 UK movie I, Monster, in
  which, bizarrely, while the other names are left largely
  unchanged, Jekyll is called Dr Charles Marlowe and Hyde is
  called Edward Blake. Christopher Lee played both in this,
  one of the best versions of the tale.
- 1971's Dr Jekyll and Sister Hyde, dir Roy Ward Baker, has Ralph
  Bates as Jekyll and Martine Beswick as "Mrs Hyde". Jekyll
  makes an elixir of life from female corpses; a side effect is
  that he periodically becomes female, his female aspect falling
  for the brother of the woman he himself craves. Oh, and he
  becomes Jack the Ripper to improve his supply of female
  corpses . . .
- Doctor Jekyll and Mister Hyde is the entirely missable 1973 US
  musical version, dir David Winters, starring Kirk Douglas in
  the dual role.
- More actively worth missing is the 1980 US movie Dr Heckyl
  and Mr Hype, dir Charles B. Griffith, with Oliver Reed playing
  the two roles. Hype is a serial killer who falls for the gal
  who's in love with the hideously ugly chiropodist Dr Heckyl.
  A Golan–Globus movie; nuff said.
- The 1981 BBC TV movie Doctor Jekyll and Mister Hyde, dir
  Alastair Reid, has David Hemmings in the dual role. A classy
  but self-conscious production.
- In the same year came the French Docteur Jekyll et les Femmes
  (vt The Strange Case of Dr Jekyll and Miss Osbourne, vt
  Bloodbath of Dr Jekyll, vt Doctor Jekyll and his Women, vt The
  Blood of Dr Jekyll, vt Le Cas Étrange du Dr Jekyll et de Miss

Osbourne, vt *Doctor Jekyll and Miss Osbourne*). Dir Walerian Borowczyk and starring Udo Kier as Jekyll and Gérard Zalcberg as Hyde, it stressed the story's eroticism and was released in the English-speaking world as if soft porn. The critic Chris Peachment commented: "God knows what the raincoat trade makes of it."

- Gloriously tasteless comedy is the aim of the 1982 updated remake *Jekyll and Hyde . . . Together Again*, directed in the US by Jerry Belson. Mark Blankfield takes the dual role.

- *The Jekyll Experiment* (vt *Dr Jekyll's Dungeon of Darkness*; vt *Dr Jekyll's Dungeon of Death*) was a 1982 US exploitationer dir James Wood and starring James Mathers as Jekyll's similarly inclined great-grandson.

- *Edge of Sanity* was a 1988 UK remake dir Gérard Kikoïne and starring Anthony Perkins. Dr Jekyll overdoses on cocaine and becomes Jack the Ripper.

- Far better is the lavishly staged 1990 US TV movie *Jekyll and Hyde* dir David Wickes, even though Michael Caine plays the dual role.

- The 1995 US movie *Dr Jekyll and Ms Hyde*, dir David F. Price, is a return to the territory of *Dr Jekyll and Sister Hyde* but set in the modern US and hammed up as a sex comedy. Tim Daly is Dr Richard Jacks, Sean Young is Helen Hyde.

- In 1996 *The Nutty Professor* was remade under the same title, this time with Eddie Murphy in the title role and Tom Shadyac as director. The sequel was *Nutty Professor II: The Klumps* (2000), dir Peter Segal.

- The 1996 movie *Mary Reilly*, dir Stephen Frears, starring John Malkovich in the dual role and Julia Roberts in the eponymous one, was based on the 1990 novel by Valerie Martin, which tells the tale from the viewpoint of a maid in Jekyll's household. Little liked on release, the movie is becoming more appreciated.

- It had to come. The 1999 US TV remake *Dr Jekyll & Mr Hyde*, dir Colin Budds, is a Hong Kong martial-arts version of the tale. Adam Baldwin is Jekyll and a butt-kicking Hyde.

- The successful Broadway stage musical spawned the 2001 US TV movie *Jekyll & Hyde: The Musical* (dir Don Roy King, with David Hasselhoff as Jekyll/Hyde) and, indirectly, the US movie *The Dr Jekyll & Mr Hyde Rock 'n Roll Musical* (2003), dir André Champagne and with Alan Bernhoft in the dual role.

- The 2002 US movie *Dr Jekyll and Mr Hyde*, dir and starring Mark Redfield, attempts to return to the pulp-horror roots of the tale's cinematic history.

- In the same year, the US TV movie of the same title, dir Maurice Phillips and starring John Hannah, was unusual in that the transformation was solely psychological, without physical manifestations.

- 2003 saw the soft-porn lesbian version *Dr Jekyll & Mistress Hyde* (vt *The Erotic Experiments of Dr Jekyll and Mistress Hyde*), dir Tony Marsiglia. Julian Wells is Dr Jackie Stevenson and Misty Mundae (wonder if that's perhaps a screen name?) is Martine/Dawn.

- And in 2005 came the US movie *Jekyll + Hyde*, dir Nick Stillwell and starring Bryan Fisher in the dual role.

- But we should not forget such masterpieces as *Mighty Mouse Meets Jekyll and Hyde Cat* (1944), *Teenage Jekyll and Hyde* (1963) and *Gentleman Jekyll and Driver Hyde* (1950), the latter an eight-minute short in which an ordinary guy suffers a mysterious personality transformation when put behind the wheel of a car.

DUNE

David Lynch's 1984 original version of Frank Herbert's 1965 novel was one of sci-fi cinema's great disappointments, and for once a remake was a reasonable idea. When it came, in 2000, it did so in the form of a 265-minute, three-part TV miniseries, a US/Canadian/German/Italian/Czech coproduction dir John Harrison and starring Alec Newman as Paul Atreides. Visually often stunning, the production suffers from an excess of respect for Herbert's somewhat self-important novel, degenerating eventually into near-pomposity. It won two Emmy Awards, for its cinematography and special effects.

THE FLY

Kurt Neumann directed the original 1958 movie, in which an experimenter with matter transmission inadvertently blends his own bodily material with that of a fly; it was based on the 1957 short story by George Langelaan. Vincent Price was among the stars.

- The 1986 version was less of a remake than a complete reconception of the original by director David Cronenberg to create a surprisingly low-key, introspective, humanistic piece. The movie is helped by the electricity between its two stars: Jeff Goldblum as the experimenter and Geena Davis as his lover.

- The 1958 movie was sequelled by *Return of the Fly* (1959), dir Edward L. Bernds, and *Curse of the Fly* (1965), dir Don Sharp. The 1986 movie was sequelled by the vastly inferior *The Fly II* (1988), dir Chris Walas.

FRANKENSTEIN

Whole books have been written about the countless movie versions of Mary Shelley's seminal sf novel *Frankenstein, or The Modern Prometheus* (1818), with their sequels, spinoffs, parodies (like 1957's *I Was a Teenage Frankenstein*), updatings (like 1991's *Frankenstein: The College Years*), analogues (like 1985's *Re-Animator*, based on an H.P. Lovecraft story), and so on. For an in-depth survey, try *The Illustrated Frankenstein Movie Guide* (1994) by Stephen Jones. Here our list is very selective indeed.

- What really kicked the whole saga off was James Whale's 1931 movie *Frankenstein*, one of the classics of sci-fi cinema (see page 20). Boris Karloff was the Monster, and his Hollywood career thereafter never looked back (or, for that matter, up). Universal sequelled this movie with *Bride of Frankenstein* (1935), dir Whale, *Son of Frankenstein* (1939), dir Roland V. Lee, *The Ghost of Frankenstein* (1942), dir George Waggner, *Frankenstein Meets the Wolf Man* (1943), dir

Waggner, *House of Frankenstein* (1944), dir Paul Malvern, *House of Dracula* (1945), a Dracula–Frankenstein's Monster–Wolf Man teamup dir Malvern, and *Abbott and Costello Meet Frankenstein* (1948), dir Robert Arthur.

- After a gap, Hammer took up the baton in 1957 with *The Curse of Frankenstein*, dir Terence Fisher. This was based largely on Shelley's novel, and had Christopher Lee as the Monster. It was followed by *The Revenge of Frankenstein* (1958), dir Fisher, *The Evil of Frankenstein* (1964), dir Freddie Francis, *Frankenstein Created Woman* (1967), dir Fisher, *Frankenstein Must Be Destroyed* (1969), dir Fisher, *The Horror of Frankenstein* (1970), dir Jimmy Sangster, and *Frankenstein and the Monster from Hell* (1973), dir Fisher.

- The first of the Japanese treatments of the story was *Furankenshutain Tai Baragon* (1965; vt *Frankenstein Conquers the World*; vt *Frankenstein and the Giant Lizard*; vt *Frankenstein Versus the Giant Devil Fish*), dir Inoshiro Honda. These were more like Godzilla movies with a different monster.

- The 1973 Spanish movie *El Espíritu de la Colmena* (vt *The Spirit of the Beehive*), dir Victor Erice, is quite possibly the most beautiful movie associated with the Frankenstein canon. In Spain in 1940 a little girl seeks solace from Franco's repression by believing in the goodness of Frankenstein's Monster, eventually conjuring it into brief existence.

- By contrast, the 1973 Italian/French movie *Andy Warhol's Frankenstein* (vt *Carne per Frankenstein*; vt *The Devil and Dr Frankenstein*; vt *Flesh for Frankenstein*; vt *The Frankenstein Experiment*; vt *Up Frankenstein*; vt *Warhol's Frankenstein*), dir Paul Morrissey and Antonio Margheriti, was essentially an extended sick joke.

- After much that had been garbage, an effort was made in 1973 to rehabilitate the story's reputation with the UK miniseries (and derived movie) *Frankenstein: The True Story*, dir Jack Smight. This had an all-star cast; Michael Sarrazin was the Creature. The aim was black comedy, and in this the production succeeded. Despite the title, the story was very substantially revised; set in England, it includes much about the Monster's proposed Bride.

- 1974's *Young Frankenstein*, dir Mel Brooks, is probably sci-fi's best-loved parody.

- The beautifully made 1975 Irish/Swedish movie *Victor Frankenstein*, dir Calvin Floyd, attempts to translate Shelley's story faithfully to the screen. Per Oscarsson was the Creature.

- The 1986 movie *Gothic*, dir Ken Russell, uses a Stephen Volk script to recreate in somewhat orgiastic fashion the night at the Villa Diodati when Mary Shelley dreamed the dream that sparked the novel.

- Dir Roger Corman, *Frankenstein Unbound* (1990) unfortunately turns the quirky 1973 sf novel by Brian Aldiss on which it was based into schlock.

- The 1992 US TV movie *Frankenstein: The Real Story*, dir David Wickes, is an excellent rendition of Shelley's novel. Randy Quaid is the Monster.

- For the big screen, *Mary Shelley's Frankenstein* (1994), dir and starring Kenneth Branagh, is another classy production, undermined by self-consciousness and some poor performances (Branagh's included). Robert De Niro is a good Monster.

- Another fine ancillary movie is *Gods and Monsters*, dir Bill Condon in 1998. Ian McKellen stars as director James Whale, depicted during his final days as he both tries to escape from his Frankenstein movies and is psychologically much reliant upon them.

- There were two US TV movies called *Frankenstein* in 2004. The first of these, dir Kevin Connor, was another essay at bringing Shelley's novel to life on the screen; Luke Goss was the Creature. The second, dir Marcus Nispel, depicted Frankenstein still alive after two centuries and now living in the USA; intended as a pilot for a weekly series, it was based on a concept by Dean Koontz and (uncredited) Kevin J. Anderson, who withdrew themselves (as did Martin Scorsese) after "creative disagreements" with the production company.

GULLIVER'S TRAVELS

At least eight movies have been based on Jonathan Swift's 1726 novel, most of them using only the first or first two voyages.

- The first of note was the 1923 French black-and-white silent movie *Gulliver chez les Lilliputiens* (vt *Gulliver in Lilliput*), dir Albert Mourlan and Raymond Villette. Even earlier were the 1902 French movie *Le Voyage du Gulliver à Lilliput et chez les Géants*, dir Georges Méliès, and the 1903 Spanish movie *Gulliver en el País de los Gigantes*, dir Segundo de Chomón, about which virtually nothing is known.

- *Novyy Gulliver* (vt *The New Gulliver*), appeared in 1933 from the USSR; dir Alexandr Ptoushko and A. Vanitchkin using puppets in stop-motion animation, it was intended primarily as a satirical attack on capitalism.

- The 1939 US animated movie *Gulliver's Travels* was the Fleischer Brothers' response to Disney's *Snow White and the Seven Dwarfs* (1937), and covers only the Lilliput voyage. Though the story is weak, the movie is still very watchable. Alas for the Fleischers: Disney had already beaten them to it with the nine-minute animated short *Gulliver Mickey* (1934).

- Called *The Three Worlds of Gulliver*, the 1959 US/Spanish version, dir Jack Sher and with effects by Ray Harryhausen, has as its three worlds Lilliput, Brobdingnag and our own world. Gulliver's fiancée Elizabeth joins him in Brobdingnag, where they marry in what proves to be a shared dream. Swift as schmaltz.

- The 1966 Japanese animated feature *Garibah No Uchu Ryoko* (vt *Gulliver's Travels Beyond the Moon*; vt *Space Gulliver*) cheerfully extends the scope of our hero's voyages. Fun, but no Oscar contender.

- The widely available 1976 Belgian/UK live-action/animated version, dir Peter Hunt and starring Richard Harris, is marked by poor animation and a tedious script.

- The 1981 Austrian/UK/US TV movie *Gulliver in Lilliput*, dir Barry Letts, was derived from a TV serial/miniseries.

- The Spanish animated movie *Gulliver's Travels Part 2* (vt *Land of the Giants: Gulliver's Travels Part 2*), dir Cruz Delgado, is a sequel to the Fleischers' 1939 movie; in this adaptation it is made clear that Brobdingnag is not a dream figment but lies in an alternative world.

- Easily the best version to date has been the 1995 US/UK TV miniseries, released also in movie form, dir Charles Sturridge. All five voyages are covered in the three-hour movie, which also focuses on Gulliver's misadventures at home: he is telling his tales from the madhouse. Among the stars are Ted Danson (Gulliver), James Fox, Sir John Gielgud, Kate Maberly, Peter O'Toole, Omar Sharif, Mary Steenbergen (Mary Gulliver) and Alfre Woodard. A magnificent production, with splendid special effects.

INVADERS FROM MARS

The original 1953 movie was the last to be dir William Cameron Menzies and exists in two versions: the shorter US release, in which at the end all is revealed to have been a dream, and the preferable European one, in which no such easy Hollywood cop-out is entertained. A small boy observes that adults, including his parents, are being changed when they investigate the site of a crashed flying saucer. It proves to be occupied by a Martian that is mentally enslaving them. (There are similar scenes in 1994's *The Puppet Masters*.) All is told as from the child's viewpoint. The unnecessary 1986 remake, a Golan–Globus production, was dir Tobe Hooper, and is faithful to the plot of the original (to the point of reproducing some scenes which in Menzies's version were added as padding) but seemingly incapable of comprehending its ethos: atmosphere was sacrificed to expensive special effects.

INVASION OF THE BODY SNATCHERS

Three movies have been based on Jack Finney's 1955 novel *The Body Snatchers*, with a fourth scheduled to appear shortly.

- The first, in 1956, was *Invasion of the Body Snatchers*, dir Don Siegel. This was one of the most significant movies of

Hollywood's paranoia era, the Pod People standing in for communists.

- The first remake, under the same title, was released in 1978 and dir Philip Kaufman. This version is a darkly comic satire, its point being that in the modern USA it can often be difficult to tell Pod People from unaffected human beings.
- Abel Ferrara's version, *Body Snatchers* (1993), transplanted the story to a military base and is one of the great actioners of sci-fi cinema, but again has a satirical subtext – indeed, two. The first is the more obvious one: the enforced uniformity of military life means human beings can become but a whisker away from Pod People. The second, more interesting, is that to adolescents the adults around them can seem like Pod People, and that this analysis is not necessarily inaccurate.
- Scheduled for release in 2006 is a further remake, dir Oliver Hirschbiegel.

KING KONG

The original 1933 movie *King Kong* is a classic of sci-fi cinema; unlike *Frankenstein* (1931) and despite the iconic nature of the giant ape, it has escaped having a myriad of bad remakes and sequels. But there have been a few . . .

- A bad sequel – bad enough that the publicists were driven to describe it as "a serio-comic phantasy" – was hurried out within months of the original to capitalize on the latter's success: *Son of Kong* (1933), dir Ernest B. Schoedsack. Karl Denham discovers another, younger ape.
- Various non-Kong movies have over the years been released under titles that exploit the giant ape's fame: *King Kong Versus Godzilla* (1963), dir Ishirø Honda, and *King of Kong Island* (1968), dir Roberto Mauri, are two such.
- The long-inevitable first remake came in 1976: *King Kong*, dir John Guillermin. Although heartily disliked by many, this movie's reputation is improving. It received a Special Oscar™ for its visual effects.

- This was in turn given a bad sequel, but this time after a dignified gap: *King Kong Lives* (1986), again dir Guillermin.
- In 2005 came the latest remake, dir Peter Jackson, fresh from the enormous success of his *Lord of the Rings* trilogy.

LITTLE SHOP OF HORRORS

The original 1960 version, dir Roger Corman, is a masterpiece of black comedy and low-budget exigencies: the script was written in a week by Corman and Charles Griffith and the movie was shot in two days because the shop set, left over after the completion of another movie, was scheduled for demolition.

- The comedy musical remake, dir Frank Oz in 1986 and based on the stage musical by Howard Ashman and Alan Menken, is ironically less funny than the original it seeks to spoof.

LORD OF THE FLIES

Dir Peter Brook in 1963, *Lord of the Flies* has had its critics but served as a complete enough cinematic statement in its own right. The gratuitous remake, dir Harry Hook, came along in 1990. Here the English public-school choirboys are replaced by US military-school cadets, so that the main point of the novel and earlier movie is lost from the outset: it becomes an adventure/horror story, and a rather clumsy one.

- A planned 1970s adaptation of the novel, to be produced by Kenneth Tynan, dir Seth Holt and with screenplay by Nigel Kneale, was unfortunately abandoned in the early stages.

THE LOST WORLD

Sir Arthur Conan Doyle's 1912 *The Lost World*, in which Professor Challenger and his cohorts venture to an inaccessible plateau where they discover prehistoric creatures still thrive, was first filmed as a silent in 1925, with director Harry O. Hoyt. The special effects were by Willis H. O'Brien.

- The 1960 remake, dir Irwin Allen, was a fairly typical Irwin

Allen creation: a goodish cast of second-string stars struggle with a banal script, and are upstaged by the special effects (done by L.B. Abbott).

- In 1992 Timothy Bond directed a mid-budget Canadian remake that, while no Oscar nominee, was good cheery fare with a good cast.
- Bob Keen directed a low-budget remake in 1998, perhaps in response to the use of Doyle's title for the second *Jurassic Park* movie in 1997. The special effects were by Louis Craig.
- Richard Franklin directed the 1999 remake as a TV movie, the pilot for the successful 1999–2002 TV series. The special effects were done by Matt Sloan (animatronics) and others.

THE LOVE BUG

The 1968 Disney original, dir Robert Stevenson, was about a Volkswagen car (Herbie) that has a mind of its own and makes its new owner a drag-racing star. Various Disney sequels followed. In 1997 came the inevitable remake, done again by Disney but this time for TV and, unfortunately, lacking the original's zest.

THE MIDWICH CUCKOOS

John Wyndham's 1957 novel *The Midwich Cuckoos* was first filmed as *Village of the Damned* in 1960, with director Wolf Rilla, which was a fairly faithful rendition of the novel but was regarded as plodding.

- A remake followed with surprising swiftness: *Children of the Damned* (1963; vt *Horror!*), dir Anton M. Leader. The latter moves the story out of the small village of the novel – the alien children pop up all over the world and are gathered together by UNESCO – and, unlike in the book and first movie, depicts them as essentially benevolent, hated solely because of human bigotry.
- In 1995 John Carpenter remade *Village of the Damned* with a cast including Christopher Reeve, Kirstie Alley, Mark Hamill and Linda Kozlowski.

THE MYSTERIOUS ISLAND

At least five movies have been based on the Jules Verne novel *L'île mystérieuse* (1874–5) in which Confederate escapees discover the remote island where Captain Nemo is hanging out.

- The first version was a US production directed in 1929 by Benjamin Christensen and Maurice Tourneur and finished by Lucien Hubbard. John Barrymore plays Nemo, here mysteriously renamed Count Dakkar. Release was considerably delayed because, after the movie had been made as a silent, MGM decided it had to have sound, and so the entire soundtrack had to be dubbed in.

- The 1941 Russian version (*Tainstvenni Ostrov*, vt *Mysterious Island*), dir B.M. Chelintsev and E.A. Penzlin, stuck fairly closely to Verne's original.

- In 1951 appeared the US 15-episode serial version, dir Spencer G. Bennett. The main addition to Verne's plot was a beautiful alien – played by Karen Randle and supposedly from Mercury – whose plans to blow up Earth with radioactive ore must be thwarted by Nemo (Leonard Penn) and the Confederates.

- Dir Cy Endfield, the 1961 remake was designed primarily as a showcase for the stop-motion effects by Ray Harryhausen. The Confederates thus encounter not just Nemo (Herbert Lom) but lots and lots of big monsters – oh, and two female castaways.

- The rather dull 1972 Italian/French/Spanish coproduction, titled *L'Isola Misteriosa* (vt *The Mysterious Island*, vt *The Mysterious Island of Captain Nemo*) was dir Juan Antonio Bardem and had Omar Sharif as Nemo.

NOT OF THIS EARTH

The 1956 original was one of Roger Corman's best sci-fi outings, with Paul Birch as an alien sent to drain blood from humans and send it back to his home planet, and Beverly Garland as the nurse who, treating him, begins to wonder if there's something strangely, well, *wrong* about her patient.

- In 1988 Jim Wynorski directed the first remake, starring Arthur Roberts as the alien and Traci Lords (better known for her porn career) as the nurse. So derivative is this remake that it drags in excerpts from some of Corman's other movies.
- In 1995 Corman himself executive produced a further remake, this one dir Terence H. Winkless with Michael York as the alien and Elizabeth Barondes as the nurse. In keeping with the changing times, this version is yet gorier than the previous two.

ON THE BEACH

The 1959 original, dir Stanley Kramer and based on the 1957 novel by Nevil Shute, is one of sci-fi's standards; it is not especially good, but its anti-nuclear-arms-race message, however muddily conveyed, still resonates, and of course it has an exceptional cast – including Fred Astaire, Ava Gardner, Gregory Peck and Anthony Perkins.

- The 2000 remake was directed as a US TV three-part miniseries by Russell Mulcahy (of *Highlander* fame). Although criticized for slowness, it's a significant improvement on the original, recreating the characters as genuine people and thereby conveying Shute's intended message far more clearly. Of especial note is the portrayal of the mixed feelings of the Australian survivors towards the American submariners: on the one hand the submariners represent humanity's sole hope of survival, on the other it was the US that pushed the nuclear button.

PLANET OF THE APES

Very loosely based on Pierre Boulle's satirical 1963 novel *La planète des singes* (vt *Monkey Planet*), the 1968 original, dir Franklin J. Schaffner and starring Charlton Heston, immediately established itself as a sci-fi classic, and was sequelled four times.

- In 2001 came the remake, also called *Planet of the Apes*. Dir Tim Burton, it was effectively a remake of the first two of the original series. Countless plot holes and a general lack of conviction led to its rejection by critics and audiences alike.
- The sequels to the 1968 original were *Beneath the Planet of the Apes* (1969), dir Ted Post, *Escape from the Planet of the Apes* (1971), dir Don Taylor, *Conquest of the Planet of the Apes* (1972), dir J. Lee Thompson, and *Battle for the Planet of the Apes* (1973), also dir Thompson.
- A 1974 live-action TV series, *Planet of the Apes*, and a 1975–6 animated TV series, *Return to the Planet of the Apes*, were based on the original.
- *Planet of the Erotic Ape* (2003), dir Lou Vockell and released directly to DVD, apparently comprises filmed sequences by diverse strippers cobbled together with a frame in which a male astronaut finds himself on an all-woman planet.

QUATERMASS AND THE PIT

The 1967 Hammer movie (vt *Five Million Years to Earth*) dir Roy Ward Baker and starring Andrew Keir as Quatermass is rightly regarded as a highpoint of sci-fi cinema. Few viewers, especially in the US, realize it is effectively a remake of a 1958–9 BBC TV series, also called *Quatermass and the Pit* and also scripted by Nigel Kneale; André Morell played Quatermass and Rudolph Cartier directed. Although the series, which has been collated into a three-hours-plus movie, definitely shows its budgetary and production limitations – it was broadcast live – it uses its extra time and even those very limitations to build up tension to levels unimagined by the big-screen remake.

ROLLERBALL

The 1975 original, dir Norman Jewison and starring James Caan, with screenplay by William Harrison based on his own 1973 story "Roller Ball Murders", was no classic, but that didn't prevent the 2002 remake, dir John McTiernan and starring Chris Klein. Even the presence of Jean Reno couldn't salvage this one. "[A]n incoherent mess, a jumble of footage in search of plot, meaning, rhythm and sense" was how critic Roger Ebert characterized it. Audiences agreed in droves.

SOLARIS

Andrei Tarkovsky's moody, evocative 1971 classic *Solyaris* (vt *Solaris*), based on Stanislaw Lem's 1961 novel of the same name, was remade in the US in 2002 by director Steven Soderbergh, with George Clooney as Kelvin. An impressive movie in its own right, it was deeply respectful of the old in terms of ambience – a still from one could easily be mistaken for a still from the other.

THE STEPFORD WIVES

Ira Levin's short 1972 satirical novel was first filmed in 1975 by director Bryan Forbes, with Katharine Ross memorable in the central role. In 2004 along came the dumbed-down remake, dir Frank Oz and with Nicole Kidman in the Ross role. Despite colossal publicity hype, it sank like a lead balloon.

* Stepford completists should look out for the 1980 TV movie *Revenge of the Stepford Wives*, the 1987 TV movie *The Stepford Children*, the 1996 TV movie *The Stepford Husbands*, and the 2001 direct-to-video documentary short *The Stepford Life*, about the making of the original.
* *The Stretford Wives*, directed for the BBC by Peter Webber in 2002, was a serio-comic serial about three sisters in Stretford, Manchester, UK.

THE TIME MACHINE

The first movie based on H.G. Wells's 1895 novella was dir George Pal in 1960. Although an enjoyable adventure, the movie discards the elements of social commentary so important to Wells's original tale, and also his pessimism about humankind's social and evolutionary future.

* A 1992 Indian remake dir Shekhar Kapur was abandoned due to inadequate financing.

- The 2002 remake was dir Simon Wells, a name that might have seemed to augur well. The time machine of a 19th-century inventor hurls him 800,000 years into the future, where he finds the Eloi and Morlocks. So far so good. But then this degenerates into excruciating trivialization in a welter of Hollywood excess and "improvements" on H.G. Wells's tale.

THE THING

The 1951 movie based on Don A. Stuart's (John W. Campbell Jr's) 1938 short story "Who Goes There?" and dir Christian Nyby and an uncredited Howard Hawks, is regarded as one of the great monster movies (see page 22). But it ignores a central element of Campbell's story: that the carnivorous alien is a shapeshifter capable of precisely mimicking the personnel of the remote Antarctic station as it picks them off one by one. This flaw was rectified in the 1982 remake, dir John Carpenter.

TWENTY THOUSAND LEAGUES UNDER THE SEA

Jules Verne's 1870 novel has been filmed many times, as has its 1874–5 sequel *The Mysterious Island* (see page 69).

- The first version was almost certainly *Twenty Thousand Leagues Under the Sea* (1905; vt *Amid the Wonders of the Deep*). Unfortunately, no credits for it are known.
- Little is known either about the first remake, Georges Méliès's *Vingt Cents Milles Lieues sous les Mers* (1907).
- A silent version was made at feature length by Stuart Paton, *20,000 Leagues Under the Sea* (1916).
- The next of real note, heralding Verne's emergence from copyright constraints, was the Walt Disney production *20,000 Leagues Under the Sea* (1954), dir Richard Fleischer and starring James Mason as Nemo, Kirk Douglas as Ned Land, and Paul Lukas as Aronnax.
- The Rankin–Bass studio released an hour-long animated version under the same title in 1973.
- The year 1997 saw the TV movie *20,000 Leagues Under the*

Sea, dir Michael Anderson and with Ben Cross as Nemo, Paul Gross as Land, and Richard Crenna as Aronnax.

- The same year saw a better-received TV miniseries, under the same title, dir Rod Hardy and starring Michael Caine as Nemo, Bryan Brown as Land, and Patrick Dempsey as Aronnax.
- Yet a third version that year was _Crayola Kids Adventures: 20,000 Leagues Under the Sea_, dir Michael Kruzan and with Adam Wylie as Nemo.
- The French TV movie _Nemo_ (1970) was based on Alexandre Rivemale's play that was in turn based on Verne's novel. The screen version was dir Jean Bacqué and starred Michel Le Royer as Nemo, Lucien Barjon as Aronnax, Jean Franval as Ned Land, and Fernand Guiot as Hetzel.
- A related TV movie is the German production _Nemo taucht auf_ (1965), written and dir Peter Hamel, and starring Hubert Suschka as Kapitän Nemo and Hans Karl Friedrich as Aronnax.

THE WAR OF THE WORLDS
The first movie adaptation of H.G. Wells's 1898 novel was produced in 1953 by George Pal, with Byron Haskin as director (see page 23). The setting was shifted to 1950s California; the tripods became, for budgetary reasons, flying-saucer-type craft; and the plot was radically altered.

- The US TV series _War of the Worlds_ (1988–90; vt _War of the Worlds: The Second Invasion_), supposedly sequelled the 1953 movie but was really just a rehash of series like _The Invaders_ (1967–8).
- Three movies based on Wells's novel appeared in 2005. The most prominent, dir Steven Spielberg and starring Dakota Fleming, Miranda Otto, Tom Cruise and Tim Robbins, was a blockbuster affair having little to do with Wells's original – just for a start, the invaders are not from Mars!
- _H.G. Wells' War of the Worlds_, dir David Michael Latt, went straight to DVD, and appears to have been an attempt to capitalize on the Spielberg release.

- Far more interesting, albeit far more flawed, was the independent movie *The War of the Worlds*, dir Timothy Hines; it is extremely faithful to Wells's novel. Starring semi-amateur actors and shot on a minuscule budget, the project had been a labour of love for Hines over several years, being temporarily abandoned in the wake of the 9/11 terrorist attacks and then restarted just in time to be completely submerged in the hoohah surrounding the Spielberg release. The acting is often poor and the budgetary restrictions are only too obvious, but the movie has gathered adherents through its ... *integrity*.
- Also of interest is the TV movie *The Night that Panicked America* (1975), dir Joseph Sargent, dramatizing the public reaction to Orson Welles's 1938 radio play based on the Wells novel.

For Centuries, We've Searched for the Origin of Life on Earth.
We've Been Looking on the Wrong Planet.
Mission to Mars (2000)

THE GIANT
TURKEY INVASION

Of course, there are plenty of dire movies – turkeys – that have nothing to do with sci-fi, but the genre does seem to attract the breed.

Fantasy cinema, too, has its share of turkeys, but those are outwith the scope of this book. Hence no mention here of movies like *Dungeons & Dragons* (2000), *Scarecrow* (2003) and *Van Helsing* (2004). *Xanadu* (1980) crept in because it proved impossibly hard to leave it out. And neither *The Matrix Reloaded* (2003) nor *The Matrix Revolutions* (2003) proved, on second watching, quite bad enough for full-scale turkeyhood.

1956: **BRIDE OF THE MONSTER** (vt *Bride of the Atom*)
Dir Edward D. Wood Jr
Bela Lugosi as mad scientist trying to turn humans into superbe-ings using an "atomic-ray" machine and bedevilled by the sad fact that his experimental subjects keep dying on him – all save one, who is turned into a giant octopus.
*   The police chief in the movie is never seen without a parrot on his shoulder. This is because the actor concerned was in real life an entertainer at kids' parties, the parrot featured in his act, and part of his deal with Wood was that he be allowed the self-promotion.

1959: PLAN 9 FROM OUTER SPACE
(vt *Grave Robbers from Outer Space*)
Dir Edward D. Wood Jr

Widely regarded – and much loved – as the worst sci-fi movie ever released (although this status is debatable: competition is stiff), *Plan 9* was another from Ed Wood. The plot – typical of the paranoia trend in US sci-fi movies of the 1950s and after – involves aliens (for which read "communists") invading the Earth and resurrecting human corpses as their zombie slaves.

- Wood owned about two minutes of unused footage of Bela Lugosi, whom he could thus claim as *Plan 9*'s star even though Lugosi had died. For the rest of the movie the Lugosi part was played by Wood's wife's homoeopathist. Unfortunately the homoeopathist didn't look at all like Lugosi; he thus performs throughout holding his cloak in front of his face. Sadly this does nothing to conceal the fact that he would have dwarfed the dead star he replaced.
- Bizarrely, the movie is dedicated to the memory of the Russian astronautics pioneer Konstantin Tsiolkovsky.
- Wood continued the revived-corpses theme in his follow-up, *Night of the Ghouls* (1959), which is about as bad but less funnily so. A fake psychic discovers the hard way that he has some genuine powers, and the resuscitated dead wreak a terrible vengeance on him for disturbing their slumber.

1962: EEGAH! (vt *Eegah! The Name Written in Blood*)
Dir Arch Hall Sr

One of the taglines for this movie tells you perhaps more than you wanted to know: "Eegah Had Never Seen a Girl Until One Fell Into His Arms! Boy Fights Giant for Girl Prize! Desert Dune Buggy First Time on Screen!" An awakened seven-foot-tall caveman terrorizes San Antonio.

- The title role was taken by Richard Kiel, who went on to play Jaws in the Bond movies. Kiel's other sci-fi appearances include *The Phantom Planet* (1961), *The Human Duplicators* (1965), *Brainstorm* (1965), *Phoenix* (1979), *L'Umanoide* (1979; vt *The Humanoid*) and *Inspector Gadget* (1999).

1968: THEY SAVED HITLER'S BRAIN
Dir David Bradley

At the end of WWII the Nazis spirited Hitler's living head off to South America; from there it has ever since been directing Nazi operations worldwide. The movie is a conflation of two quite separate halves filmed years apart and spliced together into some marginal semblance of coherence in the editing studio; the earlier-filmed part was drawn from *Madmen of Mandoras* (1963; vt *Amazing Mr H*), which had a similar plot. Unfortunately, the earlier footage, done by Stanley Cortez – of *Magnificent Ambersons* (1942) and *Three Faces of Eve* (1957) fame – is to a completely different standard from the rest. But that's only the start of the movie's problems . . .

1971: BEWARE! THE BLOB (vt *Son of Blob*)
Dir Larry Hagman

Either a sequel to or an attempted send-up of the earlier "classic" monster movie *The Blob* (1958) – it's hard to tell. Hagman managed to persuade stars like Burgess Meredith and Shelley Berman to take on cameo parts in an attempt to liven things up, but the tactic failed miserably.

* Hagman was a recognized comic actor before he took on the role of J.R. in *Dallas* (and arguably even then).

1975: THE GIANT SPIDER INVASION
Dir Bill Rebane

A black hole impacts Earth, landing in a farmer's field. Radiation from it mutates spider eggs, which hatch out as enormous spiders. This would have been risible enough in a 1950s B-movie, but as a product of the 1970s it's almost incomprehensible.

* Oops #1: An expert astronomer, lecturing on the likelihood of alien lifeforms, shows a slide of "another galaxy just like our own" . . . which unfortunately is a photo of the Trifid Nebula, not a galaxy at all.
* Oops #2: The impacted black hole makes a neat little crater, at the bottom of which it sits.

- Oops #3: Plenty more where these two came from.
- The movie stars Barbara Hale, famed as Perry Mason's TV sidekick Della Street.

1977: DEMON SEED
Dir Donald Cammell

Q: How does a computer impregnate a woman? A: With great difficulty, since computers lack male sex cells and indeed male generative organs. This doesn't stop rogue computer Proteus IV from raping and impregnating Julie Christie in a movie that succeeds in being worse than the 1973 Dean Koontz novel upon which it's based.

- Directors can often be wrong about their work, but Cammell is reported to have described it shortly after completion as "shit".

1977: THE END OF THE WORLD .
Dir John Hayes

Aliens from the planet Utopia come to Earth and take on the form of a Roman Catholic priest and a group of nuns in order to destroy our world because it's too polluted. Christopher Lee plays the priest.

1978: ATTACK OF THE KILLER TOMATOES!
Dir John De Bello

Often cited as an example of sci-fi turkeys by the ignorant, this is in fact a parody of the mutant-creature-feature subgenre: gigantic sentient carnivorous tomatoes assail San Diego before being thwarted by a teenage hero.

- Sequels have been *Return of the Killer Tomatoes!* (1988), *Killer Tomatoes Strike Back!* (1990) and *Killer Tomatoes Eat France!* (1991).
- The animated TV series *Attack of the Killer Tomatoes*, based in fact on *Return of the Killer Tomatoes!*, screened in 1990.

- The video game *Attack of the Killer Tomatoes!* was released in 1992.

1978: **PLANET OF DINOSAURS**
Dir James K. Shea

Spacers find themselves on an uncharted planet where carnivorous dinosaurs reign supreme, and must survive until help arrives. The cast appear to be strays from a picnic rather than actors; the pacing is atrocious; the stop-motion animation of the greedy monsters is little better. A nightmare of low-budget moviemaking.

- Astonishingly, this won a 1980 Saturn Award for Best Film Produced for Under $1,000,000. Quite a *lot* under $1,000,000, at a guess.

1980: **XANADU**
Dir Robert Greenwald

A muse comes to Earth to inspire a youthful musician and a nightclub-owner in setting up a roller disco. Designed as a showcase for the singing'n'dancing virtuosity of Olivia Newton-John, and an attempt to cash in on the enormous success of *Grease* (1978). Amid the mess is one of Gene Kelly's less worthy screen performances.

1981: **HEARTBEEPS**
Dir Allan Arkush

Two domestic robots, titularly male and female, develop ... well, *yearnings* for each other, escape servitude, build themselves a robot "child" and acquire a comedian-robot as an elderly "uncle". A renowned stomach-turner.

Girls Meet Boy. Girls Like Boy.
Girl Builds Giant Robot to Smash Other Girl.
Xtracurricular (2001)

1984: RED DAWN
Dir John Milius

The USA is invaded by Soviets and Cubans after the invaders have tactically nuked the USA's missile silos. A plucky band of heavily armed young Americans, including Charlie Sheen and Patrick Swayze, take to the hills and carry on activities that would, twenty years later in invaded Iraq, be described as terrorism. Some virtues – notably the portrayal of a Sovietized USA – are largely drowned in the general rabid anti-commie survivalist wet dream.

1985: THE BRIDE
Dir Frank Roddam

Sting's acting abilities have never been his strength, although in the previous year's *Dune* they served well enough. Here, though, the woodenness of his performance as Baron Charles Frankenstein is such that in the opening half-hour of *The Bride* it's hard to persuade oneself the movie isn't a parody. A large part of the movie has nothing to do with the plot, instead being devoted to the adventures of the Monster and a friendly dwarf as circus performers. That this irrelevant subplot is the best part of the movie speaks volumes about the rest.

1985: MORONS FROM OUTER SPACE
Dir Mike Hodges

Dimwit humanoid alien tourists crash their spaceship in Britain and, despite being even stupider than humans, become media darlings in the USA. What might have made for engaging satire as a ten-minute TV sketch becomes an interminable nightmare of clumsy jokes and ill-aimed swipes when stre-e-e-tched to 97 minutes. Stars Mel Smith and Griff Rhys Jones scripted this horror, so have only themselves to blame.

1986: **HOWARD THE DUCK**
(vt *Howard ... A New Breed of Hero*)
Dir Willard Huyck

Probably the worst movie adaptation from a comic-book series, and indeed the worst LucasFilms production until *Star Wars Episode One*, this was unhelped by the repulsiveness of the character design of its protagonist. Plucked from an alternate world where ducks are the dominant species, Howard soon is a social hit on Earth, turning on and being turned on by the luscious human females who swarm around him; the movie dodges obvious practicability issues. The friendly scientist who accidentally brought Howard here soon turns, for no particular reason, into one of the self-styled Dark Lords of the Universe. A bravura performance by Jeffrey Jones as the scientist is not enough to rescue this fiasco.

- The movie was such a box-office disaster in the USA that its makers, rather than blame themselves, blamed the failure on the species of the protagonist and retitled it for overseas markets so Howard's duckness was not mentioned. Few were fooled.

1987: **SUPERMAN IV: THE QUEST FOR PEACE**
Dir Sidney J. Furie

Escaped arch-villain Lex Luthor manages to clone, from one of Superman's hairs, the super-antihero Nuclear Man in an attempt to take over the world. Superman fights Nuclear Man, then gathers up the world's nuclear missiles and throws them all into the sun. Nice allegory, shame about the literalist execution. The road to a hellish movie is paved with good intentions, and no more so than here – the good intentions being those of actor Christopher Reeve, who was persuaded to reprise the central character by being permitted to determine the storyline.

1990: **HIGHLANDER II: THE QUICKENING**
Dir Russell Mulcahy

Contradicting *Highlander* (1986), here the immortals are exiles from the planet Zeist, whose evil dictator Katana comes on whim to Earth to bump off MacLeod. Earth in 2024 is not the best place to be: a while ago MacLeod designed a shield to replace the depleted ozone layer only to see an evil corporation use the shield to tyrannize Earth. MacLeod must fight off Katana, overthrow the corporation, regenerate the ozone layer, and bring the Sean Connery character back to life briefly for no perceptible reason. Magnificent overacting by Michael Ironside as Katana is in a doomed cause.

- In an attempt to make the movie less bad, the distributors savagely cut the running time from 104 to 87 minutes, thereby destroying any coherence the plot might have had.

1995: **JUDGE DREDD**
Dir Danny Cannon

In Megacity One, motorbike-riding lawman Dredd is entrusted with arrest, sentencing and often enough execution. The original comic strip is an often biting social satire; here we have instead a clichéd action plot. There are many worse actioners, but few have so completely demolished their original's virtues.

- This was the movie that reportedly Sylvester Stallone had been wanting to make for years. The other movie he's reported to have been wanting to make for years is a biopic of Edgar Allan Poe, with himself as Poe.

1996: **DOCTOR WHO**
Dir Geoffrey Sax

The pilot for a proposed US TV series, this shifts the action from the UK to the USA ... and that just about summarizes all that's wrong with it. That the story is a vacuous series of clichés doesn't help. The incomprehension of the makers as to what makes a good Doctor Who production is encapsulated in their expenditure of vast sums on a special-effects-laden new interior for the *Tardis*.

- An "explanation" is offered that the Doctor is half-human, whereas a joy of the character has always been the double-think that, while he's manifestly human, he's not human at all.

1997: ANACONDA
Dir Luis Llosa

An Ahab-style obsessor (John Voight) is determined to catch the world's largest anaconda, and inveigles a TV crew into underwriting and accompanying him. Voight chews the scenery; the anaconda chews just about everything else. The only truly frightening moment comes when one realizes that, forty years earlier, one might have thought all this was quite good.

- The tagline – "You can't scream if you can't breathe!" – tells a lot about this late-model creature feature.
- The sequel was *Anacondas: The Hunt for the Blood Orchid* (2004).

1998: THE AVENGERS
Dir Jeremiah S. Chechik

John Steed (Ralph Fiennes) and Emma Peel (Uma Thurman) investigate plot by mad scientist August de Wynter (Sean Connery) to destroy the world by changing its weather. Had this movie stopped after its first three minutes or so, all would have been well; unfortunately, it continues for a further 86 minutes – quite a short movie for one that seems so interminably long. The strength of the TV series was its conscious artificiality and campy self-parody; these the movie achieves only in its opening throw-away setpiece.

- At one stage in production, Mel Gibson was considered for the part of Steed and Nicole Kidman for the part of Mrs Peel. Meanwhile, Diana Rigg declined a supporting role.
- The original running time was well over two hours, but in the wake of disastrous test screenings the producers savagely cut the movie in an attempt to make it less bad.

1999: **STAR WARS EPISODE 1: THE PHANTOM MENACE**
Dir George Lucas

The fans had waited over fifteen years following 1983's *Return of the Jedi*, and anticipation was high. Sigh. So sad. Possibly the dullest sci-fi movie ever granted major release, this was enlivened only by an extended race sequence, modelled on the chariot race in *Ben-Hur* (1959) and seemingly inserted solely to promote the associated video game.

*   Although the movie was highly successful at the box office, at least one book-publishing company was bankrupted by the failure to sell of the associated tie-ins.

1999: **WILD WILD WEST**
Dir Barry Sonnenfeld

A wild, wild mess. An evil genius has kidnapped the USA's top scientists and plans to assassinate President Ulysses S. Grant and take over the country. Special Agent Artemus Gordon (Kevin Kline) ropes in gunslinger James West (Will Smith) to thwart the dastardly plot. Based on the celebrated 1960s TV series, but singularly lacking its wit and charm.

*   The movie cost over $150 million to make, making it the most expensive movie of its year and the most expensive ever made by Warner Bros.
*   The movie scooped no fewer than five of the 2000 Razzie Awards, including Worst Picture.
*   Two (much better) TV movies were spun off from the 1960s series: *The Wild, Wild West Revisited* (1979) and *More Wild, Wild West* (1980).

2000: **BATTLEFIELD EARTH: A SAGA OF THE YEAR 3000**
Dir Roger Christian

Hampered from the start by the fact that it was quite faithful to L. Ron Hubbard's 1982 novel of the same name, this space opera could have been worse . . . possibly. The alien Psychlos have devastated Earth, and the remnants of humanity cling on in near-savagery. But a human called Jonnie Goodboy Tyler decides to go up against the Psychlo ruler of Earth, Terl ... The numerous errors have been exhaustively chronicled elsewhere – for example, the 1000-year-old cars whose tyres are still fully pressurized.

- An animated TV series was reportedly in production in 2002, but seems to have been abandoned.
- John Travolta originally wanted to play Jonnie Goodboy Tyler but the movie took so long to attract investors that he had to settle for the role of Terl instead.
- In 2004 *Battlefield Earth* was given a special Razzie Award as the Worst Drama of the award's first 25 years. In 2001, its eligible year, it had won Razzies for Worst Picture, Worst Director, Worst Screenplay, Worst Actor (John Travolta), Worst Supporting Actor (Barry Pepper), Worst Supporting Actress (Kelly Preston), and Worst Screen Couple ("John Travolta with anyone sharing the screen with him").
- But let us not lose sight of its other awards! In 2001 it received a coveted Dallas–Fort Worth Film Critics Association Award as, you've guessed it, Worst Picture.
- L. Ron Hubbard was the founder of the Church of Scientology. Both Travolta and Preston are ardent members of the Church.

2002: RESIDENT EVIL
Dir Paul W.S. Anderson

In a vast, maze-like underground installation, scientists and troopers try, despite its myriad technological and psychological defences, to shut down a homicidal supercomputer that has turned all the installation's occupants into flesh-eating zombies. Based on a successful video game, and with a script that seems to be merely a rerun of someone playing that game, the movie succeeds in making Milla Jovovich almost unwatchable.

- In her quest for realism in the action scenes, Jovovich injured several members of cast and crew, at one point giving director Anderson a black eye.
- The movie was originally to be directed and written by George Romero – director of *Night of the Living Dead* (1968) – but his script was rejected so he left the project.

- Continuity errors abound. Jovovich starts the mission without makeup; not only does she magically acquire it but she keeps changing the colour of her lipstick.
- The movie was originally called *Resident Evil: Ground Zero*, but the title was changed for reasons of tact after 9/11.

2003: BIONICLE: MASK OF LIGHT
Dir David Molina and Terry Shakespeare

An animated movie with appalling production standards and an incomprehensible script. Somewhere on another planet, everyone's a little Lego™ robot. The good robots have gladiator-style contests in order to see who's tough enough to face the bad robots without getting their bricks knocked off. It's a mystical time of the year. Our heroes set off on a quest ...

Astonishingly, this generated a sequel, *Bionicle 2: Legends of Metru-Nui* (2004).

2003: THE LEAGUE OF EXTRAORDINARY GENTLEMEN
Dir Stephen Norrington

Based on the comic-book series by Alan Moore. In an alternative 19th century, Allan Quatermain, Captain Nemo, the Invisible Man, Dorian Gray, Mina Harker, Tom Sawyer and Dr Jekyll/Mr Hyde are sent to counter evil genius The Fantom, who is bent on plunging the world into war. The plot then rapidly loses coherence and never succeeds in finding it again. The special effects vary from excellent to sub-mediocre. A pet peeve is that Mr Hyde is presented as a hulking monster; this could hardly have been further from the Robert Louis Stevenson character.

- A highlight of the action is a car chase through the streets of Venice.
- After finishing this movie, director Stephen Norrington – who apparently had a tough time of it – was reported as saying he would never direct another movie, ever again.

HONORABLE MENTIONS

1953: *Cat Women of the Moon* (vt *Rocket to the Moon*),
dir Arthur Hilton

1953: *Mesa of Lost Women* (vt *Lost Women of Zarpa*),
dir Ron Ormond and Herbert Tavos

1956: *Fire Maidens From Outer Space*, dir Cy Roth

1969: *Skullduggery*, dir Gordon Douglas

1970: *Toomorrow*, dir Val Guest

1983: *Space Raiders*, dir Howard R. Cohen

1984: *Dune*, dir David Lynch

1985: *Lifeforce*, dir Tobe Hooper

1987: *The Time Guardian*, dir Brian Hannant

1988: *My Stepmother is an Alien*, dir Richard Benjamin

1989: *The Alienator*, dir Fred Olen Ray

1989: *Slipstream*, dir Stephen Lisberger

1991: *The Guyver* (vt *Mutronics: The Movie*),
dir Screaming Mad George and Steve Wang

1993: *Super Mario Bros.*,
dir Annabel Jankel, Rocky Morton

1995: *Johnny Mnemonic*, dir Robert Longo

1997: *Mortal Kombat: Annihilation*, dir John R. Leonetti

1998: *Armageddon*, dir Michael Bay

1999: *Bicentennial Man*, dir Chris Columbus

2002: *Scorcher*, dir James Seale

2002: *The Matrix Reloaded*,
dir Andy and Larry Wachowski

2003: *The Matrix Revolutions*,
dir Andy and Larry Wachowski

2004: *Catwoman*, dir Pitof

*...And Remember, the Next Scream You Hear
Could Be Your Own!*
The Birds (1963)

KEEP WATCHING THE STARS: AWARD WINNERS

ACADEMY AWARDS (OSCARS)

There are Oscars™ in many categories. The following list of sci-fi movies that have been honoured by the Academy focuses only on the more relevant ones.

1932
Actor: Fredric March,
  Dr. Jekyll and Mr. Hyde

1950
Special Effects:
  Destination Moon

1951
Special Effects:
  When Worlds Collide

1953
Special Effects:
  War of the Worlds

1954
Special Effects:
  20,000 Leagues Under the Sea
Art Direction/Set Decoration:
  20,000 Leagues Under the Sea

1960
Special Effects:
  The Time Machine

1966
Visual Effects: *Fantastic Voyage*

Art Direction/Set Decoration:
  Fantastic Voyage
Documentary:
  The War Game

1967
Visual Effects: *Dr. Dolittle*

1968
Actor: Cliff Robertson, *Charly*
Visual Effects:
  2001: A Space Odyssey
Honorary Award (for makeup):
  Planet of the Apes

1969
Visual Effects: *Marooned*

1972
Visual Effects:
  Bedknobs and Broomsticks

1974
Visual Effects: *Earthquake*

1976
Visual Effects: *King Kong*
Visual Effects: *Logan's Run*

1977
Visual Effects: *Star Wars*
Art Direction/Set Decoration:
Star Wars
Cinematography: *Close
Encounters of the Third Kind*

1978
Visual Effects: *Superman – The
Movie*

1979
Visual Effects: *Alien*

1980
Visual Effects (special award):
The Empire Strikes Back

1982
Visual Effects: *E.T. –
The Extraterrestrial*

1985
Visual Effects: *Cocoon*
Supporting Actor:
Don Ameche, *Cocoon*

1986
Visual Effects: *Aliens*
Makeup: *The Fly*

1987
Visual Effects: *InnerSpace*
Makeup: *Harry and the
Hendersons*

1988
Visual Effects:
Who Framed Roger Rabbit

1989
Visual Effects: *The Abyss*

Art Direction: *Batman*

1990
Visual Effects: *Total Recall*

1991
Visual Effects: *Terminator 2:
Judgment Day*
Makeup: *Terminator 2:
Judgment Day*

1992
Visual Effects:
Death Becomes Her

1993
Visual Effects: *Jurassic Park*

1995
Visual Effects: *Babe*

1996
Visual Effects: *Independence Day*

1998
Screenplay: *Gods and Monsters*

1999
Visual Effects: *The Matrix*

2000
Foreign: *Crouching Tiger, Hidden
Dragon*

2001
Picture: *A Beautiful Mind*
Director: Ron Howard,
A Beautiful Mind
Screenplay: *A Beautiful Mind*
Animated: *Shrek*
Visual Effects: *The Lord of the
Rings: The Fellowship of the Ring*

2002
Animated: *Spirited Away*
Visual Effects: *The Lord of the Rings: The Two Towers*

2003
Picture: *The Lord of the Rings: The Return of the King*
Director: Peter Jackson, *The Lord of the Rings: The Return of the King*
Screenplay: *The Lord of the Rings: The Return of the King*

Animated: *Finding Nemo*
Visual Effects: *The Lord of the Rings: The Return of the King*
Many Others: *The Lord of the Rings: The Return of the King*

2004
Screenplay: *Eternal Sunshine of the Spotless Mind*
Animated: *The Incredibles*
Visual Effects: *Spider-Man 2*

THE BAFTAS

The British Academy of Film and Television, like its US counterpart, presents its awards in diverse categories, and is in general far more imaginative in its choices of nominees – it is in particular more open to non-English-language movies. This listing is confined to movies of sf/fantasy interest that have won the Best Picture award.

1964: *Dr. Strangelove, or How I Learned to Stop Worrying and Love the Bomb*, dir Stanley Kubrick
1980: *The Elephant Man*, dir David Lynch
1985: *The Purple Rose of Cairo*, dir Woody Allen
2001: *The Lord of the Rings: The Fellowship of the Ring*, dir Peter Jackson
2003: *The Lord of the Rings: The Return of the King*, dir Peter Jackson

The Star of Raiders of the Lost Ark *and the Director of* Alien
Take You on a Spectacular Journey to the Savage World of the Year 2019!!
Blade Runner (1982)

SATURN AWARDS

The Saturn Awards have been presented annually in a wide variety of categories, covering both cinema and television, since 1972 (before 1977 they were known as Golden Scrolls) by the Academy of Science Fiction, Fantasy & Horror Films. Here are the winners in the Best Science Fiction Film category:

1972: *Slaughterhouse-Five*, dir George Roy Hill
1973: *Soylent Green*, dir Richard Fleischer
1974/75: *Rollerball*, dir Norman Jewison
1976: *Logan's Run*, dir Michael Anderson
1977: *Star Wars*, dir George Lucas
1978: *Superman – The Movie*, dir Richard Donner
1979: *Alien*, dir Ridley Scott
1980: *The Empire Strikes Back*, dir George Lucas
1981: *Superman 2*, dir Richard Lester
1982: *E.T. the Extra-Terrestrial*, dir Steven Spielberg
1983: *Return of the Jedi*, dir George Lucas
1984: *The Terminator*, dir James Cameron
1985: *Back to the Future*, dir Robert Zemeckis
1986: *Aliens*, dir James Cameron
1987: *Robocop*, dir Paul Verhoeven
1988: *Alien Nation*, dir Graham Baker
1989/90: *Total Recall*, dir Paul Verhoeven
1991: *Terminator 2: Judgment Day*, dir James Cameron
1992: *Star Trek VI: The Undiscovered Country*, dir Nicholas Meyer
1993: *Jurassic Park*, dir Steven Spielberg
1994: *Stargate*, dir Roland Emmerich
1995: *12 Monkeys*, dir Terry Gilliam
1996: *Independence Day*, dir Roland Emmerich
1997: *Men in Black*, dir Barry Sonnenfeld
1998: TIE: *Armageddon*, dir Michael Bay, and *Dark City*,
          dir Alex Proyas
1999: *The Matrix*, dir Andy and Larry Wachowski
2000: *X-Men*, dir Bryan Singer
2001: *A.I.: Artificial Intelligence*, dir Stanley Kubrick and
          Steven Spielberg
2002: *Minority Report*, dir Steven Spielberg
2003: *X2: X-Men United*, dir Bryan Singer
2004: *Eternal Sunshine of the Spotless Mind*, dir Michel Gondry
2005: *The Incredibles*, dir Brad Bird

HUGO AWARDS

Administered by the World Science Fiction Society and voted on by
the members of succeeding World Science Fiction conventions, the
Hugo Awards are presented annually in a variety of categories, most-
ly to do with the written word. Here is a listing of feature-length
movies that have received the Best Dramatic Presentation Hugo:

1958: *The Incredible Shrinking Man*, dir Jack Arnold
1965: *Dr. Strangelove, or How I Learned to Stop Worrying and
           Love the Bomb*, dir Stanley Kubrick
1969: *2001: A Space Odyssey*, dir Stanley Kubrick
1972: *A Clockwork Orange*, dir Stanley Kubrick
1973: *Slaughterhouse-Five*, dir George Roy Hill
1974: *Sleeper*, dir Woody Allen
1975: *Young Frankenstein*, dir Mel Brooks
1976: *A Boy and His Dog*, dir L.Q. Jones
1978: *Star Wars*, dir George Lucas
1979: *Superman – The Movie*, dir Richard Donner
1980: *Alien*, dir Ridley Scott
1981: *The Empire Strikes Back*, dir George Lucas
1982: *Raiders of the Lost Ark*, dir Steven Spielberg
1983: *Blade Runner*, dir Ridley Scott
1984: *Return of the Jedi*, dir George Lucas
1985: *2010*, dir Peter Hyams
1986: *Back to the Future*, dir Robert Zemeckis
1987: *Aliens*, dir James Cameron
1988: *The Princess Bride*, dir Rob Reiner
1989: *Who Framed Roger Rabbit*, dir Robert Zemeckis
1990: *Indiana Jones and the Last Crusade*, dir Steven Spielberg
1991: *Edward Scissorhands*, dir Tim Burton
1992: *Terminator 2: Judgement Day*, dir James Cameron
1994: *Jurassic Park*, dir Steven Spielberg
1998: *Contact*, dir Robert Zemeckis
1999: *The Truman Show*, dir Peter Weir
2000: *Galaxy Quest*, dir Dean Parisot
2001: *Crouching Tiger, Hidden Dragon*, dir Ang Lee
2002: *The Lord of the Rings: The Fellowship of the Ring*,
           dir Peter Jackson
2003: *The Lord of the Rings: The Two Towers*, dir Peter Jackson
2004: *The Lord of the Rings: The Return of the King*,
           dir Peter Jackson
2005: *The Incredibles*, dir Brad Bird

RETRO HUGO AWARDS

Because there were no Hugos awarded in some years, since 1996 it has been the practice to award retro Hugos for works that would have been voted on 50 years earlier had there been any voting done. The relevant Retro Hugos awarded so far are:

1996 (for works appearing in 1945):
> *The Picture of Dorian Gray*, dir Albert Lewin

2001 (for works appearing in 1950):
> *Destination Moon*, dir Irving Pichel

2004 (for works appearing in 1953):
> *War of the Worlds*, dir Byron Haskin

THE GOLDEN RASPBERRY AWARDS (RAZZIES)

In 2004 the Razzies – Presented annually by the Golden Raspberry Award Foundation – celebrated their first 25 years with some additional awards. Here's a selected list of Worst Picture Razzies relevant to the sci-fi genre.

1986: *Howard the Duck*, dir Willard Huyck
(tied with *Under the Cherry Moon*)
1989: *Star Trek V: The Final Frontier*, dir William Shatner
1997: *The Postman*, dir Kevin Costner
1999: *Wild Wild West*, dir Barry Sonnenfeld
2000: *Battlefield Earth*, dir Roger Christian
2004: *Catwoman*, dir Pitof

In addition, *Battlefield Earth* picked up a Special Award in 2004 as Worst Drama of Our First 25 Years, while Arnold Schwarzenegger was honoured with a Special Award as Worst Razzie Loser of Our First 25 Years, having scored a whopping eight nominations without ever actually winning a Razzie.

ARCANE TEXTS: BIBLIOGRAPHY

There are plenty of reference books on sci-fi movies, but most are oriented toward illustrations at the expense of information. Several of the books listed here have as subject the genre as a whole but contain very extensive information on sci-fi cinema.

Clute, John, and Grant, John (editors): *The Encyclopedia of Fantasy,* London, Orbit, 1997

Clute, John, and Nicholls, Peter (editors): *The Encyclopedia of Science Fiction*, revised second edition, London, Orbit, 1999

Grant, John: *Masters of Animation*, London, Batsford, 2001

Hardy, Phil (editor): *The Aurum Film Encyclopedia: Science Fiction*, London, Aurum Press, revised edition 1995

McCarthy, Helen: *The Anime! Movie Guide*, London, Titan, 1996

Pringle, David (editor): *The Ultimate Encyclopedia of Science Fiction*, London, Carlton, 1996

Strick, Phil: *Science Fiction Movies*, London, Octopus, 1976

Strickland, A.W., and Ackerman, Forrest J.: *A Reference Guide to American Science Fiction Films*, Bloomington, Indiana, Tichenor Publishing, 1981 (Volume 1), 1983 (Volumes 2 and 3)

The Internet Movie Data Base (www.imdb.com) is an invaluable resource for recent information, as is Rotten Tomatoes (www.rottentomatoes.com).